Networking

Networking

Work your contacts to supercharge your career

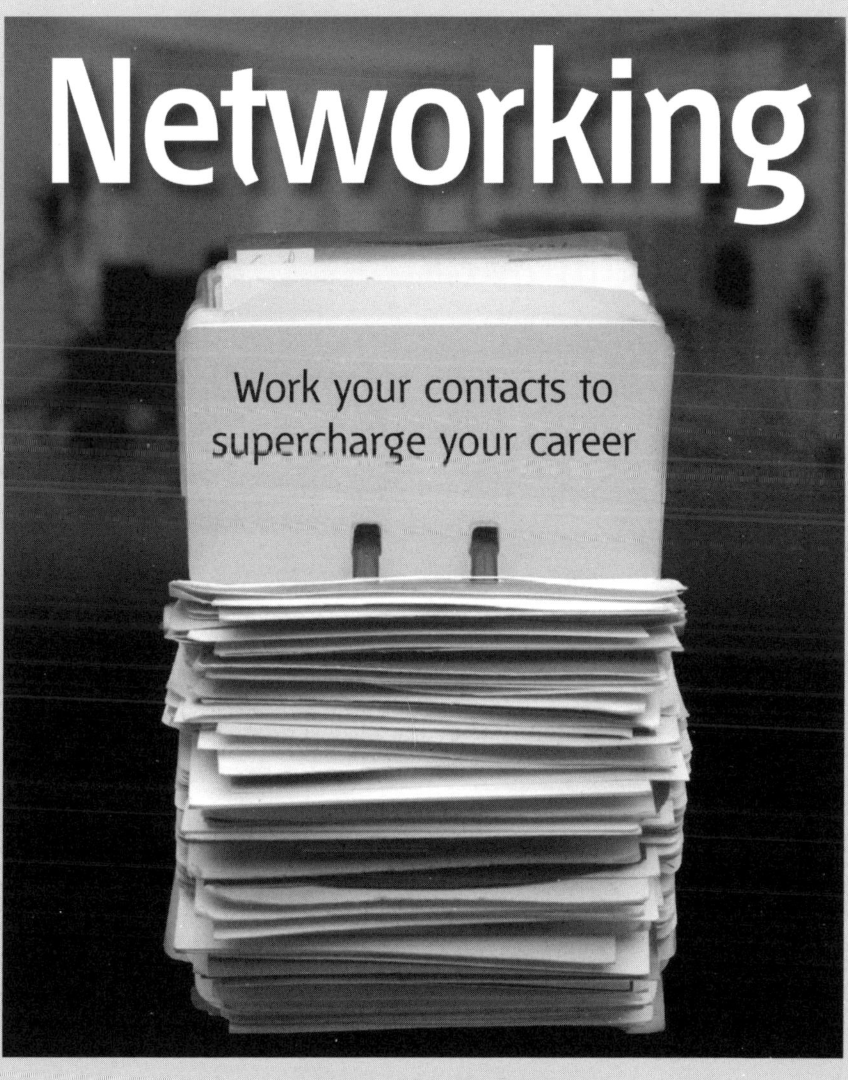

Nicolas King

Careful now
The Internet is a great resource for anyone trying to network. However, there are both good and bad sources of information online and the web is a constantly changing phenomenon. Be circumspect and bear in mind that websites change, so if you can't find the recommended link, do a search to find its new home.

Copyright © Infinite Ideas Limited, 2008
The right of Nicolas King to be identified as the author of this book has been asserted in accordance with the Copyright, Designs and Patents Act 1988.

First published in 2008 by
Infinite Ideas Limited
36 St Giles
Oxford, OX1 3LD
United Kingdom
www.infideas.com

All rights reserved. Except for the quotation of small passages for the purposes of criticism or review, no part of this publication may be reproduced, stored in a retrieval system or transmitted in any form or by any means, electronic, mechanical, photocopying, recording, scanning or otherwise, except under the terms of the Copyright, Designs and Patents Act 1988 or under the terms of a licence issued by the Copyright Licensing Agency Ltd, 90 Tottenham Court Road, London W1T 4LP, UK, without the permission in writing of the publisher. Requests to the publisher should be addressed to the Permissions Department, Infinite Ideas Limited, 36 St Giles, Oxford, OX1 3LD, UK, or faxed to +44 (0)1865 514777.

A CIP catalogue record for this book is available from the British Library

ISBN 978–1–905940–64–6

Brand and product names are trademarks or registered trademarks of their respective owners.

Designed and typeset by Baseline Arts Ltd, Oxford
Printed in India

Brilliant ideas

Brilliant features xii

Introduction xiii

1. **Feel entitled** 1
   Groucho Marx famously said 'I don't care to belong to any club that will have me as a member.' Starting with an honest evaluation of your true value will help you overcome those feelings of inadequacy.

2. **'Me PLC'** 5
   Whether you're looking for financial backers, promotion or a new job, your chances of success are greatly increased if you – and other people – have a clear idea of who you are and what you can do.

3. **Get the right mind-set** 10
   The whole idea of networking can be daunting. It just seems so pushy and calculating. Well, networking doesn't have to be that way. Here are a few simple confidence-boosting tricks to help you overcome those reservations.

4. **We're making a list** 14
   From family and school chums to suppliers and the gym – top sources for an introduction or a lead.

5. **You're my hero** 19
   Follow these suggestions and you too could meet the leaders and power brokers you admire in your field.

6. **Do your homework** 23
   Why you can't beat good, old-fashioned research for enhancing your prospects.

7. **Guiding principles** 27
   Networking is more than just swapping business cards. Here's how to make it a truly rewarding experience.

8. **Find your watering hole** 32
   Gang members, dog walkers, new mums, environmental campaigners, captains of industry – most of us like belonging to a group of people we regard as our peers. Networking makes it easier to find the right group for you.

9. **It takes two to tango** 37
   Networking is a two-way street – you have to give to get. Are you a devil of a networker or on the side of the angels? Take our quiz and find out.

10. **Cold fish** 42
    Some people are too plain busy to become your networking buddy. Sadly there are others out there who are just plain difficult – they don't want others to achieve their dreams.

11. **Soft sell** 47
    You don't have to be a pushy salesperson to network successfully but it helps if you like to talk, listen and present yourself well.

12. **The hallelujah chorus** 51
    Don't fancy blowing your own trumpet? Then recruit someone else to sing your praises. Your progress will benefit from a chorus of approval.

13. **Someone to watch over me** 56
    Look for a mentor or appoint a life-coach to help you achieve your dreams.

Brilliant ideas

14. **Wallflowers anonymous** 61
    Hate introducing yourself to complete strangers? You're not alone. Use these opening lines and tips and do it anyway, because it will help you blossom.

15. **Hotter cold-calls** 66
    Dread those first contacts? There are winning techniques that will help you get connected quickly.

16. **Be a superstar in cyberspace** 71
    A presence on career and social networking sites certainly can help raise your profile. Here's how to determine which ones are worth joining.

17. **Wear the right clothes** 77
    It's not fair but we all judge others by their appearance. Look the part and blend in with people you want to impress using our top tips.

18. **Mind your manners** 81
    Basic courtesy makes a big difference when you're trying to network and build relationships.

19. **A little flattery gets you everywhere** 85
    Brush up those interpersonal skills, like managing insecure people and defusing aggression.

20. **Good vibrations** 89
    From flirting to making new business contacts, your body language says so much about you. Understanding what your body is expressing will help you come across in an open and relaxed way.

21. **Flex that Rolodex** 94
    Whether you use traditional index cards or a brand new software package, it's important to keep track of your contacts' details.

22. **Darling, you shouldn't have!** 98
    Gift giving is a minefield. Nevertheless, the appropriate present at the right time can cement relationships and help build a resilient network of contacts.

23. **The nepotism card** 102
    Your family and their friends can open new doors and help smooth your path.

24. **Accentuate the positive** 106
    Like it or not, your reputation goes before you, so you should do whatever you can to make it work positively for you.

25. **There just aren't enough hours in the day** 111
    Don't let your busy schedule lead to lost opportunities. Try these quick and effective networking techniques for the time-poor.

26. **Make contacts before you're ready for a change** 116
    Don't wait until you're looking for the next career move. Take the initiative and establish good relationships at every stage.

27. **Masters of their craft** 121
    Don't overlook the networks that have been around for years such as your local chamber of commerce or trade association.

28. **Start your own networking group** 125
    Take the chance to display those leadership and organisational skills – it's the perfect excuse to introduce yourself to all those individuals you've been dying to meet.

29. **Power play** 130
    Corporate teambuilding and networking events can boost your profile when you grab the opportunities.

30. **The power of words** 134
    There's nothing like public speaking or writing to show you are one of your sector's leading thinkers. It's not as tricky as it sounds, either, if you stick to these proven techniques.

31. **Cast your net far and wide** 138
    Just because you're off duty doesn't mean you should be switched off – art fairs and sports venues are fabulous places to meet people.

32. **The 24/7 fallacy** 142
    Here is why putting in long, punishing hours on someone else's behalf does you no favours whatsoever.

33. **Eat your way to the top** 147
    Don't skip meals: lunch is for winners not wimps.

34. **Charitable giving** 151
    By doing charity work, not only will you help others, you could also potentially make useful contacts and learn new career-enhancing skills.

35. **Schmoozing for students** 155
    Paper qualifications aren't the whole story. Here's how to end up with something to show for your education.

36. **Make the 'freebies' pay** 159
    Get the most out of work placements and internships.

37. **Leave a clean web footprint** 164
    If the information about you on the web isn't squeaky clean, it could lose you a job – or a cherished relationship.

38. **Headhunters** 168
    To accelerate your career growth, cultivate good relationships with the top recruiters.

39. **International relations** 172
   In an increasingly globalised business world, you'll need these hot tips for networking abroad..

40. **Hosts with the most** 176
   Your business needs to get creative about corporate networking. Here are the latest trends.

41. **An affair to remember** 181
   Weddings, christenings and bar mitzvahs – there's nothing like celebrations for breaking the ice.

42. **Your other half** 185
   As high flyers and diplomats know so well, your spouse or partner could be one of the greatest networking assets you possess..

43. **They're going to find out who's naughty or nice** 189
   It's an old cliché, but how you behave at the office Christmas party could help or hinder you for the rest of the year.

44. **High-octane networking** 193
   What it takes to mix it with the big movers and shakers.

45. **Networking craft** 198
   There are well-tried techniques that can take you beyond the superficial information available from company websites and marketing brochures.

46. **Psst … don't pass it on** 202
   Skilled networkers follow the rules for handling gossip and innuendo.

47. **Staying the course** 206
   You've found the right networking groups to join. Now do your bit to keep them active and flourishing. Here's how to stop the fizz from going flat.

Brilliant ideas

48. **Losing graciously** 210
    Sometimes we just don't get our own way. Be a good loser and you'll win another day.

49. **Tackling cyber theft** 215
    The last thing you need is for someone else to benefit from your networking efforts. Take these simple precautions to help protect your online identity.

50. **Exit strategies** 220
    Learn how to move on to new pastures without burning bridges.

51. **The home front** 224
    Neighbours can be troublesome thorns in your side or reliable buddies. Follow this guide to diplomacy on your home patch.

52. **Boy meets girl** 228
    Top tips for boosting your chances with the opposite sex.

The End 233
Or is it a new beginning?

Where it's at 235
Index

Brilliant features

Each chapter of this book is designed to provide you with an inspirational idea that you can read quickly and put into practice straight away.

Throughout you'll find three features that will help you get right to the heart of the idea:

- *Here's an idea for you* Take it on board and give it a go – right here, right now. Get an idea of how well you're doing so far.

- *Defining idea* Words of wisdom from masters and mistresses of the art, plus some interesting hangers-on.

- *How did it go?* If at first you do succeed, try to hide your amazement. If, on the other hand, you don't, then this is where you'll find a Q and A that highlights common problems and how to get over them.

Introduction

It may come as a bit of a surprise but you are a natural born networker, even if your idea of the right place for a business card is at the bottom of your desk drawer. Babies and toddlers are superb at networking – so you can't say you don't know what it's like.

It's only since we started crowding into cities and learnt to keep ourselves to ourselves that we have lost the knack of relying on one another. Time pressures during the working day only add to a sense that you have to cope by yourself.

So, if you have fully developed your innate networking skills, you won't need these ideas. You might also be tempted to skip them if you are already as rich and successful as you want to be.

Otherwise, these ideas are for you. They will help you develop your natural talent for networking. They could help you get a pay rise, a new job, even a more fulfilling life.

We're not talking about the pushy and calculating pursuit of influential people who can give you an upwardly mobile hand – well, not exclusively at any rate. What we are talking about is developing mutually supportive relationships with people with whom you get on and feel comfortable.

They may be your colleagues, people in your own field or profession who you look up to, or simply your mates. They may be someone you chat to on a daily basis or a cheerleader who remains on the sidelines until you need their support.

Networking

We all need someone in our corner from time to time, so we come out for the next round encouraged that we're on the right track or patched up and equipped with some fresh tactics, energy and enthusiasm.

And *they* need your support, too. The true spirit of networking is found in two-way support. Of course, it often starts with a one-sided request for, say, advice on a particularly knotty problem at work. But a developing trust and confidence can lead to a relationship with a broader agenda.

Surprisingly, money rarely changes hands for something so useful. Most of us will help each other, when pushed – especially if there's a prospect of some help in return. So, what stops you investing time in something that could be such a help to boosting your confidence, self-esteem and career? After all, you invest in everything else, from your family and home to a good hairdresser.

'How can I find time for networking?' I hear you protest. 'I need another three or four hours in the day just to get my job done.'

Obviously you have a responsibility to do your job properly but you are entitled to a life outside work and you should prioritise some time for networking activities that will benefit your career.

That's where this title comes in. We give you practical ideas and techniques for getting the most out of what little time you can dedicate now. We tell you how to build networking activities into your routine and how to cultivate good networking habits in your daily life that will stand you in good stead in the future.

Introduction

Effective networking starts with an awareness of your own attitude to things, like asking other people for help (see 'Feel entitled' and 'Get the right mind-set'). It's important to understand the fundamentals (see 'Me PLC' and 'Guiding principles'); to be prepared (see 'Do your homework') and well-organised (see 'Flex that Rolodex').

Taking the first step is often the most difficult, like breaking the ice at networking events (see 'Wallflowers anonymous' and 'Schmoozing for students').

Polishing your social skills will help you network more effectively (see 'Mind your manners' and 'A little flattery gets you everywhere'). Applying them craftily will help you gather superior intelligence (see 'Hotter cold-calls' and 'Networking craft'). Presenting yourself pays (see 'Soft sell' and 'Wear the right clothes'), so sort out that body language and master the fear factor in public speaking (see 'The power of words' and 'Good vibrations').

As ever, the devil is in the detail (see 'Darling, you shouldn't have!' and 'Psst … don't pass it on') and perseverance pays off (see 'Staying the course').

The internet has revolutionised networking along with everything else. Leverage the power of the web and social networking sites, while protecting against the dangers that lurk on-line (see 'Be a superstar in cyberspace', 'Leave a clean web footprint' and 'Tackling cyber theft').

xv

If you are in the corporate world, you have a ready-made platform for networking. Make the most of whatever time you can dedicate to networking (see 'The 24/7 fallacy' and 'There just aren't enough hours in the day') and take a lead in developing your organisation's networking activities (see 'Hosts with the most' and 'Power play').

Don't forget to have some fun with our quiz – are you a devil of a networker or on the side of the angels (see 'It takes two to tango').

Above all, networking is enjoyable. There's not much point in establishing a networking relationship with someone with whom you don't feel a rapport – the relationship is unlikely to prosper. And it's not just about career advancement (see 'An affair to remember' and 'Boy meets girl').

Whatever you do, share your growing appetite for networking with your buddies. Oh, and do remember to tell them that they *are* your networking buddies. One City banker who had just lost her job put aside her long-held view that you shouldn't mix business with pleasure. She called around her friends to ask for help looking for a new job. They were sympathetic but largely useless. The worst moment came when an ex-colleague who she thought was one of her best friends told her to 'use her network' to find a new job.

This book contains ideas for effective networking that will help prevent something like that happening to you. If you are networking effectively, your networking buddies will know exactly how much you value the relationship. They'll know you won't take advantage of it – you can't expect more from other busy people than you are prepared to give yourself. How much you structure or formalise the arrangement is optional; respecting each other's boundaries is not. Pass it on.

1. Feel entitled

Groucho Marx famously said 'I don't care to belong to any club that will have me as a member.' Starting with an honest evaluation of your true value will help you overcome those feelings of inadequacy.

> Bring a sense of your own worth to your interaction with others. Understand what makes others want to co-operate with you and go with the flow.

Natural born networkers
You are a natural born networker. This may sound surprising, especially if your idea of the right place for a business card is at the bottom of your briefcase or handbag.

But it's only since we started crowding into cities and learnt to keep ourselves to ourselves that we have lost the knack of relying on one another. The time pressures during the working day only add to this sense that we have to cope by ourselves.

Just look at the way that pets, children and the weather bring us together. Given the excuse, we'll chat to almost anyone, as long as we recognise them as someone we can identify with and they don't seem to pose any threat.

Here's an idea for you...

Build your own fan club. Write down the names of people under three headings: those who know you; those who know your capability through your work; and finally those already in your 'fan club', who would recommend you to a friend. Brainstorm what it would take to move the people listed under the first two headings into your fan club and then act on your most promising ideas. The faster you shift them into the zone, the more powerful your network and the stronger your support.

People with a shared belief or experience are especially good at networking. New mothers have always found other new mums to chat to when out with their babies. Because they have been through something so important, they have lots to talk about and plenty of scope for further bonding. You can see the same factors at work in fields like acting, where there is an over-abundance of talent. Just about the only way of getting work in the theatre, for example, is through your contacts – which is why the family dynasties survive so strongly. In the Far East, the customary way of doing business is through your 'clan', a network of contacts a bit like a family, offering an unrivalled basis of trust and co-operation, crucial to doing business.

Don't ask, don't get

What inhibits you from exercising your natural instinct to network? Perhaps you don't like asking people for help. Don't worry unduly. You're unlikely to make anybody do anything they don't want to do. Their 'what's in it for me' radar will detect if you ask for more than they are willing to give.

Plenty of people will agree to a reasonable request, either because they are that kind of person or simply because it's easier to say 'yes' than 'no'. The degree to which people will help obviously differs and depends on the competing demands on their time and resources. However, most people have a zone within which they are willing to help members of their network. Without being part of that network, you won't ever enter their zone.

Idea 1 – **Feel entitled**

Give yourself a good rating

It's easy to believe that you are only as good as your last school report or job appraisal. But what matters deep down is not what other people say about you but what you think of yourself. Once you have that sorted out, it becomes easier to present yourself to the outside world in a way that will help you achieve your ambitions.

What's stopping you showing yourself to the world in the best possible light? Is it a feeling that you are somehow less entitled to achieve your ambitions than the next person? Think of your achievements – not just those that others have recognised but the ones that you rate highly and make you feel good about yourself. Your family; those friendships you have kept up since junior school; those good turns you did for someone; and smart decisions you made. Write them down. Go on, allow yourself to feel proud of them all.

And don't keep them to yourself. Bring that sense of your own worth to your interaction with others. Provided you are good at what you do, the more people who know you, your skills and capability, the more they will buy what you're selling and the more successful you will be.

> *Men are not prisoners of fate, but only prisoners of their own minds.*

Franklin D. Roosevelt, former president of the United States

How did it go?

Q. I've been trying to find a new job because I'm going nowhere at work at the moment. But all my attempts have come to nothing. What else can I try?

A. Give yourself a fresh start. Try a change of pace. Volunteer to work for a charity – mentoring kids with special needs, for instance. Join a dance class, choir or pottery course. If you do something you care about in a different arena, away from work, the stakes are lower and you will have a chance to restore your confidence and rebuild your self-esteem. You can return to your job-hunting refreshed and ready for the fray. You may also have added some new contacts to your network.

Q. I'm being held back at work by my lack of confidence. A friend has suggested I take drama or voice classes. What do you think?

A. Yes, give it a go as it could help you feel more grounded so that you hold your own at work more easily. Good drama or voice coaches will help you work on your breathing, which can help you present a more powerful presence if that's what you want. Some exercises will teach you how to listen and respond more spontaneously, which will improve your networking skills. Actors know what it's like to put themselves on the spot at auditions, etc., which is a useful way to learn how to put yourself across and – too often – learn about handling rejection, without taking it personally.

2. 'Me PLC'

Whether you're looking for financial backers, promotion or a new job, your chances of success are greatly increased if you – and other people – have a clear idea of who you are and what you can do.

You have a name, a reputation and probably a personal website. Think of yourself as though you were a PLC (public limited company) and manage them all together to improve your career prospects.

Many people are content to leverage someone else's brand – 'I work for L'Oreal' – throughout their careers. But as the concept of a job for life is replaced by a career made up of a number of jobs or a portfolio of business interests, it becomes more important to manage your own.

Successful brands stand for something in the minds of the people who buy into them: American Express means reassurance and customer service; McDonald's means value-for-money and predictability. If you are good at what you do and market yourself successfully, your personal brand will say something distinctive about you in much the same way.

It's a way of differentiating yourself from the competition, something that's necessary in an increasingly competitive world. Being the best is no longer enough – people have to *know* you're the best. Just think of Madonna; she's supremely good at what she does and *she makes sure we know it*.

Brand building

You should consider every aspect of who you are as part of your brand: what you do, where you're going and what makes you different. How you go about your work is just as important (e.g. with integrity, determination). If you have a skill that's in short supply, like a second language, throw that into the mix, too.

And it's not enough to simply put some words on your CV. It applies to your appearance, communication style, hopes and ambitions. The aim is that your brand should have a life of its own, creating a perception of what you are capable of doing in the minds of other people.

Rapper and business mogul 50 Cent has been quoted as saying: 'If I'm having a business conversation with some guy and we're hanging out and he's excited just to be in my world, then there's every chance he's going to sign up to something his lawyer wouldn't necessarily have wanted him to commit to.'

Here's an idea for you...

Do some reverse engineering. Think of someone that you admire – in your own industry, or maybe a completely different field? Analyse what their brand stands for and use it as a role model. Try to describe your own brand to your friends and colleagues; try out different versions until you feel comfortable describing it in a few words. Play around with it until you find a description that your colleagues will identify as you. Look for the right balance between selling yourself and being a big-head.

Adapt your brand

The management guru Tom Peters was one of the first to suggest that the idea of branding could apply to individuals as well as corporates. According to Peters, we are each the chief executive of our own brand, 'Me PLC', and ought to manage it actively. He says: 'You are in charge of your brand. Start today. Or Else.'

Of course, you can push the notion too far. For example, if you work in the public sector, an attempt at personal branding may not go down too well, as people might interpret it as brashness, the sign of a dangerous maverick.

So, adapt your brand to the expectations of your sector and the stage of your career. Do not make it too general because people won't be clear about what you do; nor too specific, as you will rule yourself out of many jobs. The more specialised your career becomes, the stronger your brand will be and the more seriously people will take you.

This is not about saying how great you are; a little modesty is essential if your colleagues are not to condemn you as a show-off or worse. Have you noticed that some of the most successful people routinely play down their own ability or intelligence with a little humour?

If you don't fancy the responsibility of managing your own brand, think about hiring a 'brand manager' to do it for you. This could be a professional marketeer or a member of your network who advises you on marketing, in return for your help on IT, say. But, don't ignore a tool that can help you take control of your career. It can help you to attract your next employer or business opportunity.

> *Personal branding is the never-ending process of making sure people know who you are, what you do and what makes you different.*
>
> Peter Montoya, USA branding guru

Idea 2 – *'Me PLC'*

How did it go?

Q. My job looks like coming to an end quite soon and I'm thinking of setting up on my own. Should I keep my personal and business branding separate?

A. It depends. For example, is your new venture B2B (business-to-business) or B2C (business-to-consumer)? Say you are currently cooking for the directors' dining room at the headquarters of an international bank and your plan is to set up a catering business. If your business will be B2B, then 'Directors Dining' might be a better bet than 'Katy Glynn', and vice versa if you'll be dealing direct with your consumers.

Q. I'm still at college and I'm struggling with the whole idea of 'Me PLC'. Isn't it a bit early for me to start defining my own brand when I'm only just setting out on my career?

A. It's never too soon to have an idea about where you're going in your career. However, you should avoid being too specific early on or you will rule yourself out of many jobs. Think about your long-term goals: perhaps you want to be the boss of a company – your own, perhaps. You'll need a variety of skills. Focus on these and develop a brand that will help deliver the experience that you need to get there.

3. Get the right mind-set

The whole idea of networking can be daunting. It just seems so pushy and calculating. Well, networking doesn't have to be that way. Here are a few simple confidence-boosting tricks to help you overcome those reservations.

Successful networking can help bring you a new job, partner or business opportunity. But the main benefit is discovering that lots of other people are what you want them to be — and you can be what they want, too.

What's stopping you?
Let's identify the reasons why you might say networking is not for you.

- It sounds so calculating; your mother wouldn't like it! Don't be so sure. She herself may be far more widely networked than you imagine. In any case, why would you let family prejudices stop you using your talents as you see fit? That's a recipe for missing out on life's opportunities.
- Maybe you think that talent will out. Sadly, an over-abundance of humility won't get you very far in a competitive environment. Those qualities of reserve and effortless success – characteristic of the gifted amateur who triumphs over all obstacles – may be admired in some quarters, but they belong to romantic novels and they won't get you promoted.

Idea 3 – **Get the right mind-set**

- It's a self-defeating exercise. If the only idea is to meet someone more important or influential than you are, any networking event is doomed to failure with at least one side of each encounter feeling dissatisfied. Well spotted! That would be true if networking was just about your upward mobility. However, it is actually about providing mutual support.

Feel the force
You won't recognise the power of networking in your career or social life before you experience it for yourself. Like a tender, loving relationship, you don't know one until you experience it.

Play a little mind-game with yourself to see if it's for you. Think about what it would mean to you if you were to find a group of people who accepted you completely for who you are. Surely you would feel comfortable sharing your ambitions, fears and dreams with them, wouldn't you?

The good news is that that's exactly what your network can bring you. Plus, it may bring you a promotion or career move along the way, too.

It does involve taking a slight risk – mainly being prepared to make yourself vulnerable by sharing your innermost thoughts – but that's the way to go if you want to put your ideas into action.

Look for early returns
So, park those reservations and get cracking. As you develop your networking skills, you will feel better about your ability to work with others, which will help build your confidence. Your self-belief will make you a passionate presenter of

Here's an idea for you...

If you are finding it tricky to talk up your own achievements and to sound polished and confident, don't worry – so do most people. Just do what other successful people do: stick with reality. Be resolutely realistic about your own accomplishments and your prospects and plans. Be supportive of other people's plans and show interest in them as people. Networking relationships will develop naturally when you come into contact with people with whom you share a common bond or interest.

your views and help convince others to buy into what you so evidently believe yourself – that you are a someone worth backing.

Be inspired

Networking is the hallmark of successful people. Take Sir David Li, a member of one of Asia's most prominent families. Even in Hong Kong's famously clubby culture, he is considered a networking legend. As the chairman and chief executive of Bank of East Asia, he is a pillar of Hong Kong's pro-China business establishment. But he uses his formidable networking skills to keep on good terms with leading members of the territory's pro-democracy movement.

He and his wife have a penthouse apartment with a kitchen they almost never use, apparently. Most meal times are an occasion for a social or business engagement. Sir David's only hobby is 'schmoozing', with business acquaintances and friends. According to one of them, 'It's very important for him to have an audience and be the host. He loves it.' Like Sir David, if you're *not* networking, you're in danger of missing a trick.

If you want to be respected, you must respect yourself. Spanish proverb

Idea 3 – *Get the right mind-set*

How did it go?

Q. I have used networking to find a new job. Can I park it now that I'm safely back in the corporate world?

A. No way! Networking is a good way to develop skills that will hold you in good stead in the corporate world. Increasingly the flatter structure of organisations means that the old 'command and control' management hierarchies are on their way out. Your ability to get on in your company now is much more likely to depend on your success at influencing people – in your own organisation as well as outside contacts like suppliers.

Q. Fortunately, I have inherited £40k. I plan to invest it in a business venture that will eventually give me a chance to become my own boss. A friend has recommended a franchise opportunity but I'm not sure that's right for me. What do you think?

A. You're absolutely right not to rush. Take a good look around before you commit your nest egg. This is when you should use your networking skills to arrange an invitation to the 'beauty parades' that business angels and investment clubs hold regularly. You will see entrepreneurs pitch for equity investors to take a share of their business and the response from experienced investors at the meeting. Then you can compare the hottest propositions against each other and the franchise deal your friend has recommended.

4. We're making a list

From family and school chums to suppliers and the gym – top sources for an introduction or a lead.

Whether you want a complete change of direction or simply to raise your profile at work, start by identifying the networks of which you are already a member.

It's the first step towards leveraging contacts that will help you achieve your career goals. You may find this hard to believe but you are almost certainly already a member of half-a-dozen networks. Some of them are so blindingly obvious that you might not have even noticed them. Others, like your friends or family, you tend to take for granted. For most people these networks include the following.

Family
Just being a relative gives you a great network to tap into – from your parents and siblings to those distant cousins in New Zealand. Together with your spouse or partner's connections, you are part of one massive family chain. These are the easiest people to approach when you need a favour – for example, when you need some extra cash – and they are usually glad to help you out.

Friends
You've been through so much together, from sharing a flat to that fabulous holiday in Greece. They helped you through a bad break-up with your ex. When

Idea 4 – *We're making a list*

you need to escape from the rat race they'll gladly ask their auntie to lend you her seaside cottage. You even trust them to tell you if that gorgeous green dress is truly flattering.

School

You have bonded in the classroom – from the girl who always sits next to you to the lecturer who lent you that book that helped you get an A. That bond will always remain even though you go your separate ways. Your college chum who became a surveyor will be the first person you talk to when you're thinking about buying a property.

Colleagues

You spend more time with your colleagues at work then you do with your own family. You experience the ups and downs of business with them. They can show you the ropes at work. They can give you a tip or contact. As a bonus, many of your professional relationships will blossom into close friendships. Who knows, you might even end up marrying the boss's daughter.

Business partners

Your companies have been doing business together for years: an accounting firm that has kept your tax bill to a minimum; a designer who did that glossy brochure for your products. Thanks to them you managed to get a discount on that Chardonnay from the wine merchant that also happens to be a client.

School gate

As a parent you bump into other parents twice a day every week during term time. Then you spend weekends ferrying your small-fry from their home to yours.

> *Here's an idea for you…*
>
> Now you do it! Write down the half-a-dozen or so networks of which you are already a member – use a separate sheet of paper for each one. Then list individuals in each network and how that contact might be able to help you (e.g. with information or an introduction that could take you nearer your next career goal). These are the people you need to get in touch with – the more of them you talk to, the more likely you are to make progress.

You can rely on them to recommend a clown for a birthday party. It's also likely they'll know exactly who to call when you're looking for a plumber or decorator.

Sports or hobby group
Right from the very beginning you had something in common – your interest in tennis or art. They have introduced you to a super little restaurant after a match or an outing. As you have got to know them better, they have somehow managed to find you seats for Wimbledon or put you in touch with a first-class framer.

Get in the swim
With most of these people, your connection is mainly social. You chat to them about their news. There's no specific agenda, just a reassuring affirmation of your relationship as relatives, friends, or colleagues. However, once you've spotted the potential of networking, you are ready to start making a little more use of these alliances. For example, next time you go to a family 'do', find time amid the chat to discuss your work with your uncle or cousin, say. They may just listen. On the other hand you may find that your cousin has some useful suggestions about one of your projects.

You probably won't produce your business card at every opportunity but if you put work and your career on the agenda, you are more likely to get some benefit from people who almost certainly want you to succeed.

> When people talk, listen completely. Most people never listen. Ernest Hemingway

How did it go?

Q. I've been networking like crazy but I'm making very slow progress. Why is it taking so long to see any results? What can I do to speed things up?

A. I'm afraid you have to expect to put in quite a bit of effort before you start seeing results. Other people are just as busy as you are and they have to see some benefit before they'll do anything for you. It's all about cultivating a relationship with them. It takes time to develop a rapport. The good news is that as you work your way up the ladder, members of your network grow more influential and you can expect things to happen faster.

Q. I've been given a new contact's address and telephone number. How do I know which is the best way to get in touch with them?

A. Use your judgement. In some fields, a letter or an email is more appropriate. For example, academics and members of local government tend to prefer an initial contact in writing. However, this can be a bit of a cop out – it's less nerve-racking to write a letter or send an email than get on the phone. It may take a couple of attempts to get hold of the person you're trying to reach, but a phone call is more likely to be effective. Then back up any arrangements you make in writing.

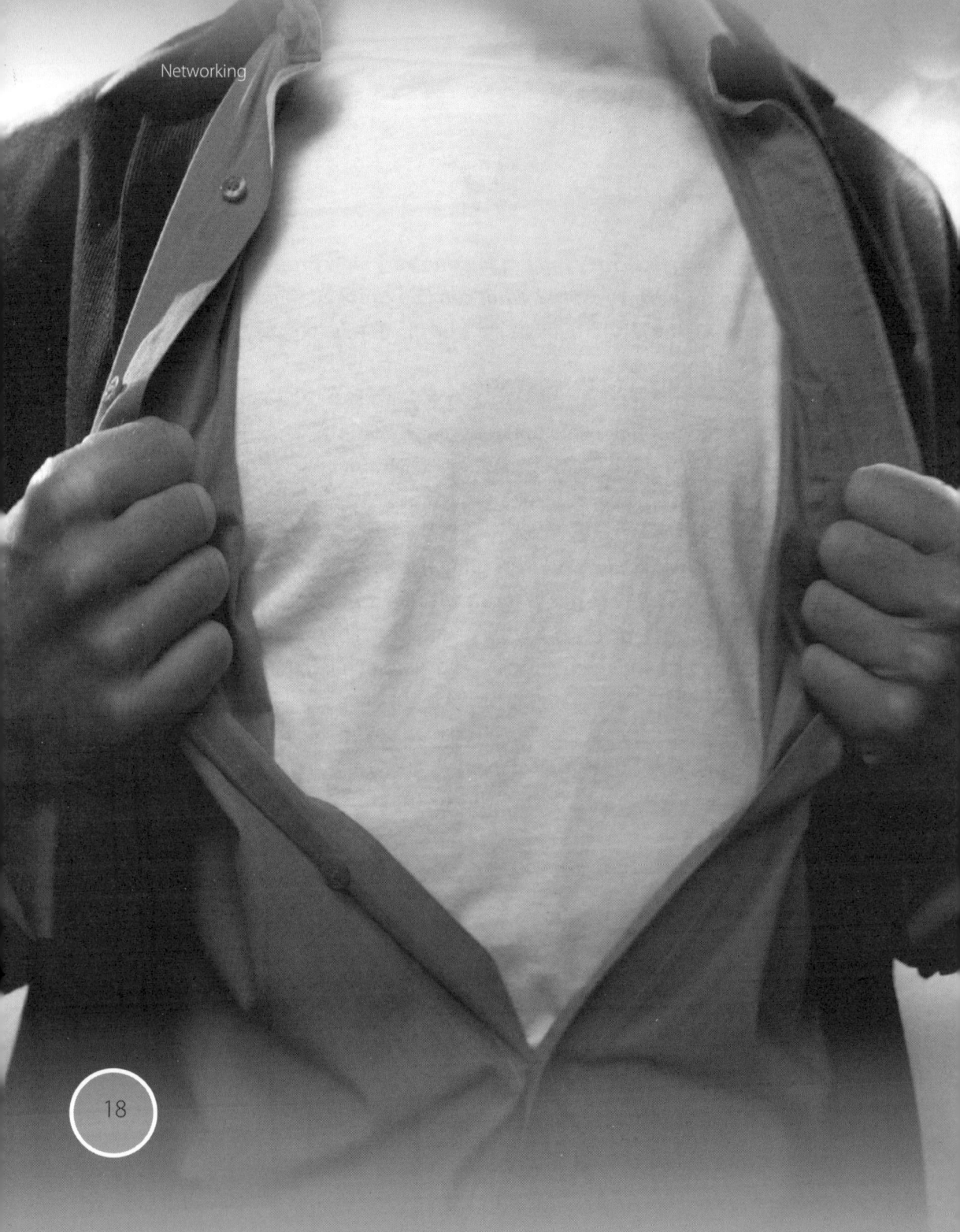
Networking

18

5. You're my hero

Follow these suggestions and you too could meet the leaders and power brokers you admire in your field.

Make the effort to meet your hero in the flesh, as the reality could change your outlook on life.

Engineers, entrepreneurs, scientists, teachers – whatever the source of your inspiration, it can galvanise your whole being. We all have childhood dreams about what we want to be when we grow up. A huge part of the process is meeting people that we admire, look up to and want to be like.

Part of growing up is coming to grips with a more realistic appraisal of what to expect from people. Our role models change or fade away. But some remain influential. It's vital that they do because few things exert such a powerful influence on our drive and motivation.

Seismic shifts

You know when a meeting with someone rocks your thinking. For Christine Comaford-Lynch, author of *Rules for Renegades*, a meeting with Bill Gates was to change her outlook on life in a fundamental way. She had always found the supreme self-confidence of billionaires seductive but when she met him the main thing that struck her was that his confidence did not come so much from wealth as from an inner self-confidence, his certainty that he would achieve what he set out to do. The reality of actually meeting him forced her to an understanding. 'I finally admitted,' she says, 'that I couldn't get it by osmosis, I would have to develop it myself.'

From zero to …
Throughout your life, you should look for every opportunity to make a realistic appraisal of potential role models. Look upon it as banking credit for your career. Once you enter the world of work, great academic results are no longer enough to ensure your progress. It's important to start developing your social network in parallel with your studies. An advantage in making contacts at this early stage is that your heroes may be more willing to indulge you due to your youth and obvious chutzpah.

For example, one architecture student we know volunteers as a host for his school's visiting speaker programme. It's a chore but part of his duty is to wine and dine the speakers, which means that each term he gets to chat with at least one distinguished member of the profession he wants to enter, in pleasant circumstances. Chances are they will remember him if he calls at a later date to discuss an internship or summer project.

Intermediate slopes
As you grow beyond your teens, your relationship with your heroes is rather more grown-up. You are still slightly in awe of them but you should just about be able to hold your own in conversation.

You can't wait for inspiration. You have to go after it with a club. Jack London, American adventure writer

Ask one of them to speak at a charitable event, such as a fund-raiser for a local museum. This does some good for the community and the positive PR can only enhance your profile. It shows that you know how to take the initiative. You will also add to your network. Soon, if you go about it correctly, you can be at the nexus of several networks of your choice – for example, business, artistic and intellectual.

Reach for the summit

When you're aiming for the keys to the executive washroom, you have to up your game. Learn how to play in the big boy's playground: go to the same bars and restaurants as members of your chosen network. Be seen at social events like gallery openings, sports games and major art exhibition previews.

Fuel your ambitions

Above all, your heroes provide fuel for your own dreams and ambitions. The main source of inspiration for June Reynolds-Lacey, founder and chairman of the Mobilefone Group, came from her grandfather who she never actually met. A family story of his success drove her on towards fulfilling her own ambitions. When she felt she had done enough to match his achievements, she finally confessed to her mother what had driven her for so many years. To her amazement her mother told her that the family story was in fact completely wrong – it was her grandmother, not her grandfather, that had the business acumen.

> **Here's an idea for you...**
>
> Learn to 'hover with intent'. You want to meet someone who is already engrossed in a conversation. Observe the group from a distance. At a natural pause in their conversation, such as a change of subject, join them. Don't immediately butt in; just listen with interest. Only introduce yourself if the body language tells you it's the right time (e.g. when someone turns to you). Address your target directly along the lines: 'I see you're busy; when's a better time for a word?'

How did it go?

Q. I am keen to interview the chairman of an engineering firm for an article I'm writing for a trade paper but his personal assistant won't put through my call. How can I get past her?

A. Have you been nice enough to this person? Part of her job is to screen calls and insulate her boss from interruptions that someone else could easily deal with. She may deal with a dozen calls like yours every day. Persist politely – maximising that charm. Don't treat her as an adversary: engage her support. Show you understand how busy she is and explain the benefits of the interview in terms of achieving positive PR. Ask her help in finding a slot in her boss's busy schedule.

Q. I run my own small computer software business. By chance I heard this graduate student speaking at a conference. Wow was she talented! How can I persuade this rising star to come and work for me when she finishes her MBA?

A. Some people are motivated by more than just money. They are looking for stimulating work, with a high degree of autonomy, which gains them rapid hands-on experience and wide-ranging responsibilities – in other words, experience that looks great on the CV and enhances their employability. So, emphasise how small businesses are often better positioned to deliver this than larger firms, which often promise the world but in practice corral their graduates in a narrow discipline.

6. Do your homework

Why you can't beat good, old-fashioned research for enhancing your prospects.

It pays to do some detective work. What you unearth about a company or a contact will give you the edge when you're networking.

Websites
The first thing you should really look at is what a business or individual has to say about themselves. This might be stating the obvious but the fastest and easiest way to access this information is by looking at their website. A company site will provide all the basics on what they do – their products and services – as well as their philosophy and company culture. If you're fortunate, there will be press releases and company reports which tell you quite a bit if you read in between the lines. It will list employment opportunities, work schemes and any charitable activities they're involved in. You can also use company websites to find the names of contacts. For example, a PR (public relations) person is often a useful first port of call.

Ask yourself what makes this company special; who are their clients? Take the time to find out their main competitors and have a look at their websites too. This will give you a much better picture of a company's position in the marketplace as well as their strengths and weaknesses.

Try an internet search engine to check for personal profiles, CVs, presentations and papers that company managers have delivered at conferences.

It's usually worthwhile to have a quick trawl of the chat-rooms and gossip forums that claim to dish the dirt on the corporate world. You never know what you might dig up. However, digest any tasty little nuggets of information you come across this way with a degree of scepticism, as they are often the opinions of disgruntled ex-employees with vengeance on their minds.

Recent research in the UK and USA discovered that more than 60% of business executives are registered with a networking site. If it's information on an individual that you're after, these sites are heaven-sent. Try sites like MySpace and Facebook or business networking sites such as Linked-in.

Impromptu snaps and comments posted on social networking sites like these can tell you quite a bit about people's personalities and are a wonderful source of topics that will engage their interest. Human resources managers now routinely use them to round out their knowledge of candidates and employees – a useful reminder that you should think very carefully about what you reveal in your own online entries.

The media
As you're aware, company websites are marketing tools – all sunshine and no rain. They only tell you what the company wants people know. For harder and more authoritative facts, mine the newspapers and trade journals both on- and offline. A look at the websites of media organisations such as the BBC and Reuters

can also be very rewarding. Be sure to obtain some background information about the company's sector too. You'll find it especially useful if there's little about the company or individual you're researching.

Face to face

By far and away the best source of information about a company or individual is to talk to someone acquainted with the business or that person. So, pick up the phone. Better yet, try to arrange a quick chat face-to-face. Insider low-down is much richer than information on the record and in the public domain. A word with the right person and you could gain insight you couldn't find out any other way. Of course, your contact will pursue their own agenda and put their own spin on what they tell you; in person, however, you can pick up information from their tone or body language. In fact, talk to several people if possible so you learn as much as you can and also to gain a number of different perspectives.

> *Here's an idea for you...*
>
> Don't forget to feed your own name and company into a search engine. When you're trying to form a mutually beneficial relationship, you have to expect that your contact is going to want to get to know you better, too. So you'll need to be aware of what others can find out about you. It will help if you anticipate questions and you're ready to answer them on a personal level (e.g. who you are, what you do, and how you could help your contact in return).

> *Knowledge is of two kinds. We know a subject ourselves, or we know where we can find information on it.*
>
> Samuel Johnson, eighteenth-century English writer and lexicographer

Networking

How did it go?

Q. We've got a brand manager coming in to pitch to my company. When a colleague checked her out online, he found some pretty compromising photos of her partying. Do we cancel the meeting?

A. Okay, it was very silly of her to post pictures of debauched extracurricular activities on the web, especially if she's brand manager of all things, but that's all she's guilty of at this stage. Don't simply judge her by what you found online. Some people play hard but still manage to be totally professional when they're at work. Did someone you trust recommend her? Have other members of your business employed her in the past? Think carefully before you cancel your meeting or you may be depriving yourselves of a first-rate talent.

Q. I've been trying to find out about my client's main competitors. None of them has a website nor has been mentioned in the media. Any other suggestions on where I could look?

A. All registered companies have to file company returns. In the UK, limited companies have to register at Companies House, which is run by the Department of Trade and Industry. You might try visiting their website, which enables you to search for rudimentary information such as office addresses, telephone numbers and names of directors. It also provides access to company documents, including company accounts and annual returns, which could prove fruitful if you're trying to keep an eye on the competition.

7. Guiding principles

Networking is more than just swapping business cards. Here's how to make it a truly rewarding experience.

Having a great network of friends and colleagues is the secret to your career and your life — it's one of the few things that can grow with you. Like anything worthwhile, you have to work at it.

Networking is all about relationships. Like personal relationships, you have to work at professional relationships to make them fulfilling. They thrive on things like trust and personal contact. There has to be some give and take. It's only when people get to know, like and trust you that there's a possibility of a real two-way street, where you can call on them and they can call on you for support.

Practice what you preach

The first relationship you have to consider is the one you have with yourself. Can you trust yourself to deliver on your commitments? Can you rely on yourself to deal with setbacks? Do you give yourself a break when you don't live up to your own high standards? Do you give yourself permission to change your mind, relax and have fun?

Here's an idea for you...

Say it in person. If most of your friends have an @ in their name, it's time to return to first principles. It's easy to confuse efficiency with effectiveness: just because you have sent an email doesn't mean you have dealt with something. Talking face-to-face helps move things along faster, especially if you have something tricky to discuss. Before you fire off your next reply, think whether it might be quicker in the long run to say it in person.

The more comfortable you are with yourself, the more meaningful your interaction with others. Treat them courteously and with respect – remember to 'treat others as you would like to be treated'.

Build solid relationships

When you meet someone, be yourself. There is no point in trying to project something that you are not – people will see through a lack of sincerity. There's no substitute for genuine interest and curiosity about people you meet. Be enthusiastic to learn more about them. Pay attention to them as people, not just what they might do for you. Listen carefully and ask questions that show your curiosity.

If you think they could become part of your network, make a note of their details. Include personal information such as the name of their partner, whether they have children; career details such as companies where they have worked; and people you know in common.

After a meeting, follow up with an email or phone call to thank them for their time, even if they haven't been any help. Always offer to try to help them in the future and invite them to contact you.

Always follow up on things you promised to do or things they undertook to do for you. Keep in touch routinely, not just when you want something. For example, send a card at birthdays and holiday times. Never forget a thank-you note when they do something on your behalf.

Don't expect too much too soon; it takes time to establish trust, an essential ingredient to a productive relationship. Talk about yourself and reveal your feelings, as this gives a cue to someone that it's okay to do the same, which establishes a rapport and an exchange of confidences.

If it's a surprise to them when you finally ask for their help or support, you have not done your job properly.

Network in-house
If you are in the corporate world, you have a ready-made platform for forming networking relationships. Find people you admire in your own organisation who can act as informal mentors; you never know when you may need them, or when they may need you. These may not be the people with whom you get on best. Mentors need to stretch you so they may be people with whom you've had the odd run-in.

Learn how to network at the right level. The most obvious connections you can make are those with your peers, people who have a similar level of responsibility and experience. Widen your net to include people higher up and lower down the pecking order. Remember that most people are used to family relationships with parents, brothers and sisters and are quite capable of relating in a variety of ways to different people at work. It might help you start off on the right foot if you anticipate how they will see you – as a big sister or a little brother, etc. – as it will help you establish a rapport with them.

> Relationships take time; they take effort; they have their own rhythm. Depending on what you put into it ... your network will be there for you.

Herminia Ibarra, Professor of Organisational Behaviour, INSEAD

How did it go?

Q. I've made some great contacts but one guy is making constant demands for emotional support for his problems and it's taking too much of my time. How can I exit gracefully?

A. Some people will play on your sense of guilt or desire to be popular to the extent that it amounts to emotional blackmail. This is not grown-up behaviour. If you're finding it tough to handle, it probably means you are not being as assertive as you could be. Whenever you feel he's asking too much of you, say you haven't the time to talk and stand your ground. Adopt the 'broken record' technique, if necessary, repeating the same phrase over and over again. If that doesn't work, try something more direct like 'Careful, that's beginning to sound like emotional blackmail' and see him back off.

Q. One of my networking buddies is always willing to help me out but I don't like asking too often because I don't want to take advantage of her kindness. Is there anything I can do to show my gratitude?

A. Be ready to help in return when she asks for your support. Meanwhile, say thanks in person and let her know what a difference her support has made. Then remember to follow up. Write her a handwritten note or card and post it promptly.

8. Find your watering hole

Gang members, dog walkers, new mums, environmental campaigners, captains of industry – most of us like belonging to a group of people we regard as our peers. Networking makes it easier to find the right group for you.

Being part of the right network — among soul-mates and kindred spirits — brings out the best in you. Here's how to tell when you've found your natural surroundings.

The media view of networking – upwardly mobile people touting their business cards – is too narrow. Networking has less to do with selling yourself, or your business, and more to do with being part of a group where you feel you belong; a valued member of a community, where members make contact, share information and support each other.

Paul Armstrong, managing consultant at career advisory consultancy Penna, Sanders and Sidney, encourages a use of networking that's not just a tool of career development but a form of mutual support.

Idea 8 – **Find your watering hole**

'People think of it as "What's in it for me?"' says Armstrong, 'but it's a two-way process: "I may want your support now but I may be able to help you out in three months' time".

'Don't just go for those that seem most useful,' he says. 'It's not just about career development: you provide soul-mate support for each other. They may have no influence over your career; they are just people you get on with.'

Like an animal that returns to a regular watering hole, you know when you've found your natural habitat. You feel relaxed and comfortable with the other people around you. You can be yourself without having to make too much of an effort.

Among your peers you will find people you can bounce ideas off, people you can help and others than can help you. You can join in and have your say but you don't feel any pressure to do so. You look forward to the next time you meet up. Above all, others can see what you have to offer and value your contribution.

Where to start
A good place to start for business networks is at your local Chamber of Commerce or government-funded business network, such as Business Link in the UK. If your industry has a trade association, try joining it. For social networks you could try joining a local group that champions a cause in which you believe; just do an online search for the key words and your post code and see what comes up.

> *Here's an idea for you...*
>
> Spread your net wider. Try a group that you might not have thought of before. Remember that you're casting around to find like-minded people. So, as long as you keep within your own comfort zone, the exact nature of the group is not that important. Sure, it's a bit hit-and-miss, but what you're looking for is worth some effort. It's a real bonus to find people who you would be pleased to meet, even if there wasn't a shared interest, such as business, charity work or learning a language.

Never mind the excuses

You might think you're a timid creature but once you find the right group, you'll flourish and grow. After you've been to a meeting or two, you will recognise a few of the regular members and start to feel like you belong.

It's only natural to feel shy about taking the first step but the benefits of networking with your peers easily outweigh the hurdles. Genuine networking is a processs of give and take: when you're in the right group, you'll discover people that, on some occasions, need your help and, on others, help you. Make life easy for yourself on a first visit with a little preparation.

- Research a few of the people that might be there in case you meet them.
- Prepare a phrase with which to introduce yourself – and practise it.
- Have a follow-up sentence ready in case someone asks you what you do.
- Listen and show interest in what people tell you about themselves.

Above all, be yourself and be considerate to other members. Recognise that it takes time to get to know someone so be courteous and patient.

Being at a club that supported me meant a lot.
David Beckham, former Manchester United star

Idea 8 – *Find your watering hole*

How did it go?

Q. Help! I'm just too shy to try a new group. Any suggestions?
A. It helps if you're introduced by someone that you already know. So try asking friends, relatives or work colleagues if they take part in some kind of local networking event, such as a local business network, community action group or evening class. If they do, don't be afraid to ask if they'd mind if you went with them to the next meeting. Tell them you're a bit too shy to go by yourself – most people know exactly what that feels like. If no one you know can introduce you, go online and look on the web for a local group that interests you. Make a few online contacts first and then once you have established some rapport and can trust them, suggest a get-together or meeting.

Q. How can I tell when I've found my 'watering hole'?
A. You'll probably recognise instinctively when you're among soulmates and feel a sense of relief that you have found a group to which you naturally belong. If you need to analyse it more carefully, consider if it passes some important tests:

- Do you look forward to the next meeting?
- Do you feel you can talk to just about anyone at any time without having to try too hard?
- Even if there was no particular focus to the group, would you still want to meet up with the people participating?
- Are the people in the group giving you what you need from them?
- Are you having fun?

If you answer 'no' to more than one of these questions, you should probably keep looking.

Networking

9. It takes two to tango

Networking is a two-way street – you have to give to get. Are you a devil of a networker or on the side of the angels? Take our quiz and find out.

See if you have that spirit of give and take that successful networking requires.

Choose answer a), b) or c) for each of the following questions. There are no right or wrong answers – just choose the one that comes closest to your own instinctive response. The results will tell you more about your attitude to networking.

1. When you leave the office at the end of the day, are you most likely to:
   a) say 'good-night' and head off home;
   b) wait for that colleague who lives near you so you can travel home together; or
   c) troop out with the crowd and head round to the local pub for a drink with them?

2. You bump into a co-worker you've had disagreements with in the past. Do you:
   a) take a deep breath, go over to her and make light conversation – perhaps you can be friends, after all;
   b) remind her why you're not talking to her; or
   c) look past her as though you haven't noticed?

3. Your 'ex' tries to contact you via your Facebook entry and asks you to give him a call. Do you:
   a) invite him to Sunday lunch to meet the family;
   b) reply that you really must get together again sometime, while resolving never to be available; or
   c) explain politely but firmly that your relationship was in the past, that you have moved on and hope that he has, too?

4. A friend of a friend asks you to meet her for a drink after work. She wants to pick your brains about opportunities to work in your sector. Do you:
   a) agree to meet but warn her you only have half-an-hour;
   b) say you don't have time to meet but you're happy to have a chat on the phone; or
   c) suggest she sends her CV to your HR department if she's looking for a new job?

5. You arrive at the office Christmas party. Do you:
   a) start talking to other people who are just arriving and join them on the way in;
   b) head straight to the free bar and stay there all evening; or
   c) head off in search of your closest colleagues so you know you'll have fun?

6. Your boss asks you to be his 'friend' on a social networking website. Do you:
   a) agree to give him access to a new page with limited details that you set up specifically for work colleagues;

b) agree happily to his request, on the basis that there is no distinction between work and play when it comes to social networking;

c) explain to him that you no longer use social networking sites because they eat into working time.

Scoring

Questions 1, 3 and 5: For every reply a) that you gave, score 1 point; for every reply b), score 3 points; and for every reply c), score 5 points.

Questions 2, 4 and 6: For every reply a) you gave, score 5 points; for every reply b), score 3 points; and for every reply c), score 1 point.

The verdict

If you scored 25 or more, you're on the side of the angels and in tune with the true spirit of networking. You understand that it's about forming relationships of trust and mutual support. But you are no soft touch – you have understood that a commitment to mutual support does not mean that you spend time on hopeless cases or lost causes.

If you scored 10–24, your experience of networking seems to have been disappointing. Perhaps you've found that others have let you down or are unwilling to go to any trouble to help you. If so, bad luck. Try lowering your

> **Here's an idea for you...**
> Do your friends a favour. Tell them about a great business deal that they can come in on or put them in touch with a great new contact, somebody that can make a huge difference to their prospects. You tend to get back what you give – although you may have to wait a while to see it and it may come back from a different source. Great networkers believe that what you give out comes back tenfold.

expectations. Just look out for people you get on with and with whom you can have a good relationship; don't just go for those who seem most influential.

If you scored less than 10, you may be a bit of a devil but at least you're honest! You're inclined to disregard the value of networking – it's simply not worth the bother. The very idea of soulmate support probably leaves you muttering about 'do-gooders'. I wouldn't like to be around the next time someone tells you 'life is about give and take'.

After first confidences between people moving towards friendship, a rest between exchanges of information somehow hastens, not impedes, the growing trust. Candia McWilliam, Scottish author

Idea 9 – *It takes two to tango*

How did it go?

Q. An ex-colleague has asked me to write him a reference pretending that I was his boss at the company where we both used to work. I would like to help but don't want to do anything dishonest. What should I do?

A. Ask him to explain why he can't ask his real boss and only agree to help if there's an innocent explanation. Stick to the truth in your letter but write what you think will promote his job chances most.

Q. I'm going to the office party and am hoping to get a chance to run an idea for a project past my boss. Do you think I should avoid mixing business with pleasure?

A. No, it wouldn't do any harm at all to show your dedication to your job by talking about work at the party. But remember to keep it relaxed. It's a social occasion and your boss will probably be busy chatting to friends and colleagues. Try to join in with their conversation and pick a moment when you can catch your boss's eye. Say you've been discussing an idea with your colleagues and would like to run it past him next day at work. He can hardly say 'no' and if he shows interest in discussing it on the spot, grab the chance.

10. Cold fish

Some people are too plain busy to become your networking buddy. Sadly there are others out there who are just plain difficult – they don't want others to achieve their dreams.

You can't do much about the fact that many people are too interested in themselves to help you. But you can learn to recognise the type and develop coping strategies for those who promise so much but deliver so little.

The blanker
You've probably experienced it at first hand. You bump into someone that you know for certain recognises you. Perhaps you even worked together briefly on a project. When you give them a friendly greeting they stare back at you impassively as if you were a complete stranger. It feels humiliating. Why did they blank you? You can think of nothing you have done to cause offence. You give them the benefit of the doubt – they could be shy – but more likely the brutal truth is that they no longer regard you as a useful contact and are chasing better offers.

The know-it-all
They assume all the authority of a professor lecturing first-year students. Their motto: 'If you want to do business with me you'll have to hear me out.' These people act as if they have the right solution to every problem and have an overwhelming desire to be recognised as someone of superior ability. They see no need to listen to a different perspective and instantly dismiss anyone who puts forward other ideas. They can be patronising, domineering or downright frustrating.

The manipulator
You've met a charming business contact. Talks are going well. Then suddenly you find yourself on the wrong end of a deal. These individuals are silken tongued and as slippery as eels. Manipulators are masters at twisting conversations, specialists in half-truths and selective omissions. The annoying thing is you can't actually prove that they're being manipulative because they never leave any evidence.

The highly strung
It seemed like an incredibly promising meeting at the time. But now that you have followed up, you realise your contact is a bundle of nerves. They are demanding and easily offended. Their conversation is peppered with outbursts. Working with them is like treading on eggshells.

Here's an idea for you...

Reach for the comfort blanket. If you are thin-skinned and prone to tears after a stressful situation like dealing with someone difficult, distract yourself so you don't break down so easily. Walk away, have a drink of water and give yourself a moment to recover. Remind yourself that this will pass. Imagine the person who hurt your feelings stark naked in public or some similarly humiliating scenario. Find a sympathetic soul for a comforting chat or a hug.

The character assassin

What did you do to upset them? You think you've established a good working relationship with someone when, out of the blue, you hear from a colleague that they are blaming you for a problem, such as a delay or unsatisfactory standard of work. These people seem to spend their lives looking for an opportunity to make someone look bad because – they believe – that will make them look good. Their vicious comments don't usually produce results; they just annoy people.

What can you do?

Working with difficult people is hard and time-consuming but you may have no choice. The first thing to recognise is that if you find someone difficult to deal with, you won't be alone. They are usually so much into themselves and give so little thought about anyone else that everyone has a problem with them.

You'll never change them, but in a way that makes your life easier. Difficult people are predictable people. How often have you heard someone say 'Oh, don't bother asking her, she'll never help'?

They are stuck in their ways, which gives you the chance to handle them effectively. Work out what makes them difficult. What do they actually want? If they are a stickler for detail, give them detail – loads of it. A 'know-it-all'? Listen to them attentively and keep telling them how right they are.

Don't try to beat them at their own game – you'll never win. Nor is it a good idea to confront them, as they will simply deny any intention to be difficult. Indeed, they may be totally unaware of their behaviour. The truth is we're all capable of being difficult. At times we might behave in any or all of these 'difficult' ways ourselves. If you learn how to recognise the signs, you'll be able to understand 'difficult' people better and set more realistic expectations for your networking activities.

Curious things, habits. People themselves never knew they had them. Agatha Christie

How did it go?

Q. I keep meeting this warm and friendly banker at events. She always offers to help me then never follows through. What's going wrong here?

A. Everyone likes to feel popular and accepted but some people take it to extreme levels. They love attention and want everyone to be their friend. To win you around they'll tell you things you want to hear. Your banker friend sounds suspiciously like one of this type. Her neediness is causing her to make promises only to let you down by not delivering. If you really need her help then ask her to explain the underlying issues which are preventing her from taking action. Be ready to compromise so you can get what you want and she can save face.

Q. Our marketing director can be quite sarcastic. He's always dishing out back-handed compliments. Do I put on a brave face and just ignore him?

A. Why should you allow all his belittling nonsense to eat into your sense of self-worth? You can be gracious but you're not obliged to let someone walk all over you. Stand up for yourself but don't fight mud with mud. Keep your voice calm, your expression sweet and your attitude good humoured. Ask him to back up any critical comments with facts – here's betting he won't have any. Otherwise offer an amused but forgiving retort. You probably won't change him but there's an excellent chance that he'll back off.

11. Soft sell

You don't have to be a pushy salesperson to network successfully but it helps if you like to talk, listen and present yourself well.

Here are some sure-fire ways to market yourself to best advantage.

There is more than one way to sell yourself in a networking situation. You do not have to try to be like that stereotypical, pushy and ambitious salesperson you see in the movies. However, it helps if you like talking to people. And you *do* need to believe in what you're doing if you want to influence them. If you are not excited about it, why should anyone else be?

You are your number one customer

Of course, there's one person who has to be wholeheartedly convinced that you're worth backing before you try to persuade anybody else – and that's you. If you are less than 100% convinced, people will pick up on your doubts and will be less than convinced themselves.

Tell your story. Show your passion for what you are doing. Give people something to connect with and if it chimes with their own experience they will engage with you. It's your energy and enthusiasm that will carry them along with you and spark their interest in working with you or buying your product or service.

Networking

Here's an idea for you...

Anticipate people's objections. Think about the reasons that people will be negative about you, your product or your service. Think of all the problems you would face working on a project with someone and how you would overcome them together. Then you will be able to deal with people's objections as your probing questions unearth them. What's more you will feel confident and able to talk with complete conviction.

Look the part

Dress as if you are already on the same team as your networking contacts. People relax when they are among their peers and are more likely to open up to someone who is reassuringly like them. If in doubt, opt for a smart outfit. For men, it's easier to take off a tie to fit in with the dress code for an event than to put one on when you arrive. Being female can be an advantage – you can dress to impress so that you stand out against the hordes of men in suits.

Listen to what they want

Ask them what they are currently working on themselves. Show your interest by listening attentively and asking questions that show you understand what they are telling you. When you see the chance, ask questions that allow them to open up on their favourite subject, which in most cases will be themselves. Have some questions ready for a suitable occasion.

- 'How did you get into this type of work?' This invites them to share their story with you, so listen attentively.
- 'What do you like best about what you do?' This allows them to give a positive response and feel good about themselves.
- 'In what way are you and your business different from the competition?' This is an open invitation to brag.
- 'What's happening in your sector?' This positions them as an expert in their line of business and makes them feel important. You might learn what skills or products will be needed in the future, which might give you a hook for your discussion.

Idea 11 – **Soft sell**

One step at a time
Ask them where they are with their plans and where they want to get to next, such as the next stage on a project or major milestone with a business venture. Listen for any sign that they are looking for help and any buying signal that hints that they would be interested in your help.

Explore their current needs or future plans with them. If you think you can help, make suggestions for how you could work with them to achieve their plans. Focus in on the benefits that working with you or your company will bring them, such as doing things faster, better or cheaper.

Above all, show your enthusiasm for whatever project you're talking about. You have to believe in its value – they won't buy into your story unless you do. Make the running until they start to see the benefits of your proposition, which will spark their imagination and allow you to work jointly to identify the next steps. Logic alone is not enough – work on a blend of reason and emotion.

> It is well to remember that the entire population of the universe, with one trifling exception, is composed of others.

Andrew J. Holmes, American physician and author of *Wisdom in Small Doses*

How did it go?

Q. I'm not the natural networking 'type' and I'm definitely not a salesperson. Are there skills that I can learn to compensate?

A. Yes, you don't have to be a 'natural' to succeed. You can learn most of the communication skills you need from a business coach or drama teacher. But to network successfully it definitely helps if you are genuinely interested in other people and like talking to them. If you're the kind of person who prefers almost anything to making new contacts and hates chatting to people socially, then networking might not be for you.

Q. Sometimes I feel that other women that I meet look more polished than me and that puts me at a disadvantage. Any tips?

A. You can be sure that when powerful women expect to meet other powerful women, they will reach for their wardrobes. To make an impact, raid the safety-deposit box for your best jewellery. Allow ample time for make-up. Load on the accessories: gloves, financial newspaper, iPod, BlackBerry and, of course, your designer sunglasses.

Q. I'm pretty good at developing a rapport with new contacts but it seldom leads to anything concrete. When is the right time to ask for the business?

A. How blatantly you ask for that business or job is a matter of personal style – most people are slow to ask. Look for early buying signals such as an interest in talking about the kind of help you could give. Test the water with a question such as 'should we be following up on this together?' Strike as soon as you sense the other party is ready to make a commitment – and eliminate the competition.

12. The hallelujah chorus

Don't fancy blowing your own trumpet? Then recruit someone else to sing your praises. Your progress will benefit from a chorus of approval.

Find people to say nice things about you and you don't need to say so much yourself.

Many people are uncomfortable talking about themselves and their achievements. They see any attempt to promote themselves as pushy and vulgar. They believe that their careers should be an apparently effortless progression; a just reward for talent and hard work.

As a blueprint for success, that leaves a lot to chance. For most people, being good at what they do is not enough – they need every advantage to climb the career ladder, including their own PR. Despite this, they still can't bring themselves to push themselves forward.

If it goes against the grain to shout your own worth, you could think about finding help from a professional career coach who can work with you on presenting yourself; or from one of your networking buddies who is a whiz at branding and self-promotion. Ideally, find someone with good contacts in your sector, with an ear to the ground for what's happening and who is recruiting currently.

Here's an idea for you...

Be public spirited. Doing something on top of your work or home life can help you stand out from the competition. Join a public body or become a school governor. The bonus is that public bodies have to be accountable – they have to publish information about their activities and membership. This means that someone doing an online search for background information on you will come across your name in relation to your public duties, which could give you an edge in career situations.

A recommendation carries more weight

Finding people to say nice things about you scores highly, too. What's more, you don't have to spend so much time on your own PR and you can concentrate on your work. A third party's recommendation always seems to carry greater weight than your own efforts. It's a truism that you are more likely to believe something you read in an article in the paper than in the advert alongside it. Similarly, companies looking for staff or clubs looking for members all attach a lot of credibility to other people's recommendations.

The best way to be spotted for a new job is by someone else putting your name forward. While there's nothing to stop you cold-calling an agency or headhunter, it's better by far if someone recommends you. One experienced headhunter explains: 'The bulk of what we do is sourcing. This is where we call people and ask them who they recommend. We keep a large network of informants and we cross-check all the information they supply.'

Tune up the orchestra

Of course, people will only mention your name in glowing terms if they know you are good at what you do. They'll be even more inclined to oblige if they know they can rely on you to do the same for them in similar circumstances.

Idea 12 – **The hallelujah chorus**

It's up to you to earn a reputation among your colleagues through your ability and hard work. Then you have to keep everybody up to date on your progress and achievements. Each time you have something to report, such as when you are promoted or complete a successful project, send a customised letter or email message with the good news to each one of your network buddies. Don't overlook friends and acquaintances you have built up over the years – scour those school yearbooks, address books and party invitations for their names.

Turn up the volume
In fields such as writing, sport and showbiz it's customary to have an agent – a good one is worth their weight in gold when it comes to securing a good contract. But whatever your sector, you can probably think of people who would help if only they knew of your ambitions (e.g. satisfied customers who would give you a testimonial to post on your website; or a supplier of products that are complementary to your company's who would pass on sales leads for a commission). You can do something similar outside work, with support from friends, relatives and other people who know you well, such as team mates from your sports club. Sometimes, all it takes is to sit down together to discuss the benefits and spell out any incentive. If you can agree on something that suits you both, suddenly there's a multiplier effect on your own efforts.

Never look down on anybody unless you're helping him up. Jesse Jackson, American politician

How did it go?

Q. I'd like to encourage my networking buddies to suggest my name if a headhunter asks them for a recommendation. Is it appropriate to offer an incentive?

A. There's no future in offering money. Nobody whose recommendation is worth having is going to suggest your name in return for payment – they have their own reputation to protect. However, you should tip off members of your network to expect a call and tell them how important this job is to you. Then if it comes down to them recommending you or someone else and there's little to choose between you in terms of capability, they'll give you the nod.

Q. I expected my boss to recommend me for promotion but far from being my chief booster he never seems to give me credit for my achievements. Is there anything I can do?

A. Others will have noticed if your boss has a bias against certain people, so check with colleagues to make sure you're not imagining it. Then ask your boss for a meeting to discuss your prospects. Keep it calm and see if he has any specific criticisms, which you can address. You should also take every chance to work with influential people within your organisation who could champion your claim to be promoted.

Idea 12 – **The hallelujah chorus**

13. Someone to watch over me

Look for a mentor or appoint a life-coach to help you achieve your dreams.

Mentoring is a very powerful tool that gives you feedback on your ideas and personal advice on where you're going with your career.

Do you remember a teacher who inspired you at school or college; someone who helped you out when you were struggling with a particularly knotty academic problem or even gave you some advice about your love life?

If you do, then you know what it is to be mentored. We all need someone in our corner from time to time, so we come out for the next round encouraged that we're on the right track or patched up and equipped with some fresh tactics.

Mentoring is a very powerful tool – four out of five successful candidates for promotion have had mentoring from a member of their company's senior management team. A mentor will usually give you feedback on your ideas and – if they know you well enough – personal advice on where you're going with your career.

Young people can no longer count on this kind of advice, which extended family networks used to provide. Women, particularly working mothers, need advice on how to juggle their time without hampering their progress at work. Talk to successful entrepreneurs and you almost always find there's at least one important figure in their lives who has shown belief in their ability.

On the ranch
You can usually find yourself some mentoring in a large company, if you look for it. Certain people will stand out as having a little more experience or knowledge and seem willing to find a bit of time for you now and again. Grab them before someone else does because potential mentors can make all the difference to your career.

The relationship is something like a friendship with a bonus. You can draw on your mentor's experience and understanding of your situation to step back from the daily grind and think about your options. Sometimes you may find it easier if your mentor is slightly outside your own patch at work – for instance, you can enjoy a franker exchange if your mentor knows your boss but has a different reporting line.

Here's an idea for you...

If you work for yourself or just want some incognito advice, e-mentoring may be the answer. There are a number of services on the web you can sign up to. It is rather like online dating, only you post your individual business issues and wait for a response from mentors who think they can help. Because both parties remain anonymous, secrets remain secret and if you don't hit it off you can move on without any awkwardness.

Horses for courses

Surprisingly, money rarely changes hands for something so useful. If the mentoring takes place between people who work for the same employer, the mentor is usually happy to give advice for free on company time or over a drink after work.

At the highest levels, some senior managers and captains of industry pay someone to help them improve their performance at work. They may opt for a business coach to work with them on things like motivation and leadership skills. A good coach knows how to ask the right questions and help their clients find their own answers, so they can move forward with their endeavours. Mentors work more from their own experience.

Michele Jobling, who works as a professional mentor, says that she is most definitely a mentor and not a coach. 'A mentor combines business expertise with coaching attributes while coaches tend to come from a psychology background,' she says. She was previously a retail consultant and is herself a former chief executive. 'We are business people,' she adds. 'We have seen the good, the bad and the ugly, so we can help clients.'

Happy mentoring relationships

Trawl carefully through your own personal network to see who might be the right mentor for you. The key to the relationship is that you get on well together – it should be an enjoyable process for both of you when you meet. Once you've found one, do not take them for granted; your mentor is not at your beck and call and is not a psychotherapist. Listen to their advice but take responsibility for your actions yourself.

> Mentoring is to support and encourage people to manage their own learning in order that they may maximise their potential, develop their skills, improve their performance and become the person they want to be.

Eric Parsloe, the Oxford School of Coaching and Mentoring

Networking

How did it go?

Q. I have just reached a more senior position than my mentor. Is it time to find a new source of advice?

A. The answer depends on whether or not you honestly think you still receive plenty of support and sound guidance from this individual. If the relationship still works for the two of you, there is no need for any change. Great mentors, like great teachers, are often less successful then their pupils. Take Sir Keith Joseph, credited today for promoting the career of Margaret Thatcher, Britain's first woman prime minister.

Q. Sometimes when my mentor challenges me I feel really irritated. How do I respond without losing my cool?

A. At times, even constructive criticism can be hard to take. Well, swallow your pride. Acknowledge that you have taken their comments on board – that's all people want really. Privately you may dismiss their advice but it doesn't cost you anything to say you appreciate their concern. Then take action if their point is valid or do nothing if you disagree – the choice is yours.

Q. I am moving to New York but I would still like to maintain my relationship with my mentor. Any tips?

A. Finding that special someone you trust to bounce ideas off isn't that easy. Fortunately you've got a great connection going already and there's no reason why you shouldn't continue to keep in regular contact by phone and online. When you come back home for visits catch up face-to-face.

14. Wallflowers anonymous

Hate introducing yourself to complete strangers? You're not alone. Use these opening lines and tips and do it anyway, because it will help you blossom.

The thought of arriving at a function full of people and having to talk to them might rank as your worst nightmare, right up there with public speaking or making a presentation. But it doesn't have to be scary.

Nowadays, we're all so used to email and text messaging that face-to-face conversation, especially with strangers, can leave us feeling awkward and tongue-tied.

The key is to be yourself at all times and considerate to others – they are probably just as nervous as you are. In fact, the more you stay in touch with what's going on around you and try to put others at their ease, the better your networking results will be.

Here's an idea for you...

Practise initiating conversations so that when you meet new people at networking events it becomes second nature. Get used to doing this in everyday situations like queuing at the supermarket checkout – a smile is often a clue that someone is willing to interact with you. You're not trying to be clever, just passing the time of day. Extend your range beyond talking to people you see frequently, like neighbours, colleagues or waiters. And beware: it's not true that every tourist or elderly person likes nothing better than a bit of a chat, although many do.

Be prepared. Try to do a little research on one or two of the people you expect to be at the event so you are prepared when you meet them – ask the organiser who is likely to attend. Also, rehearse a selection of one-line introductions about who you are and what you do, so you are ready for when you meet someone new.

There's no substitute for genuine enthusiasm and curiosity about the people you meet. Listen attentively and ask questions that show you're interested. Strike the right balance: a natural intimacy takes time to develop, even between people with a lot in common, and people can feel overwhelmed if you're too pushy or inquisitive. Talking about yourself, revealing your feelings, gives a cue to someone that it's okay to develop the conversation along personal lines.

Almost everyone likes attention, so show interest in them as a person, not just for what they do. Keep the conversation moving: ask if they're finding the event useful; tell them what you thought about one of the speakers and ask what they thought.

Top tips to help you blossom

- *Arrive on time*. Once an event is underway, it's sometimes tricky to catch the mood and energy level. If you arrive late, you have less in common with the those who were present for the talk or presentation that you missed – and, therefore, less to talk about.
- *Start to mingle as soon as you arrive*. If you don't see anyone you know, head for a group of three or more people. Don't try to interrupt; just fall in with their conversation and show interest through your body language until there's a natural opportunity to introduce yourself.
- *Smile: be approachable and enthusiastic*. Make good eye contact with everyone you talk to.
- *Stay in touch with what's going on around you*. Try to put others at their ease. Imagine you're a host: introduce yourself and people you recognise from previous meetings. Bring newcomers into the conversation with a 'We were just talking about …' greeting.
- *Be realistic*. You're there to network not to make instant friends. That doesn't mean you focus exclusively on what you want to get out of someone. Networking is a two-way street and you're there to help and support each other. If you make two or three good new contacts at each networking event, you're doing OK.

Classic opening lines: 'Mind if I join you? I'm new here', 'Didn't I read something you said about …?' 'You work for Tesco? I'm a serious fan of your bakery.'

Classic exit lines: 'Great to meet you, good luck with your plans', 'It's really interesting to talk to you; do you have a business card?' 'You two really should be talking to each other.'

> Networking is about connecting with your heart to leave a lasting memory. The best networkers create relationships first and, as a result, commerce follows. Penny Power, founder Ecademy

Idea 14 – **Wallflowers anonymous**

How did it go?

Q. I always seem to get trapped talking to someone boring; if it's someone interesting, they always seem to waltz off and leave me. Is there any way to tell when it's time to move on?

A. Follow your instincts. If it's hard to get a word in edgewise with a bore try to rope another networker into the conversation and scoot. Alternatively, wait for a suitable moment, smile, shake hands and as you move off, wish them luck with their plans. If you're really getting on well with someone, don't be in a rush – it's not a competition. Just don't take it personally if they waltz off first. Take a moment to quell that childhood fear of abandonment and reconnect with what's going on around you. New groups will have formed and you can join one.

Q. What about business cards – are they really necessary these days?

A. Lots of people prefer to keep their BlackBerry or mobile phone handy at networking events so they can swap contact details on the hoof. But we reckon you should still bring business cards with you. They are versatile. You can pop a note on a card to remind yourself or your contact what topic you were discussing together and any action points. They are also a handy prop – producing a card can act as signal that you are about to move, giving your contact the opportunity to do the same.

65

15. Hotter cold-calls

Dread those first contacts? There are winning techniques that will help you get connected quickly.

Let's face it, calling complete strangers and asking for favours scares most people. There's real pressure on you to make a great impression — instantly — while you're feeling vulnerable and exposed.

Okay, the whole idea of cold-calling is about as appetising as eating a swarm of bees. However, you should be aware that experts say the telephone is one of the most effective means available to find a job. One successful call could be all that stands between you and achieving your goals. This makes the telephone a networking tool you just can't ignore. And the good news is that there are ways of minimising the sting in the cold-call process.

As any sales whiz knows, you can generally talk to any person you want to if you go about it the right way. The idea is that you are never more than six 'degrees of separation' from any person on the planet if only you know how to join up those steps. Here's how it works.

You are one step away from a person you know and two steps away from someone that they know ... and so on. Get each person to introduce you to the next until you reach your chosen contact. Then your call will be far from cold and the response warmer than you might imagine.

Getting in shape to make those calls
Old hands do plenty of preparation so they feel less panicked and their self-esteem doesn't automatically hit zero when they receive a knock-back. Before you even reach for the phone follow these steps:

- Produce a short snappy outline of what you plan to say so you don't get tongue-tied. Make sure you include the name of the person who referred you to the contact.
- It's important to have a list of questions prepared just in case the person you are calling has time to talk. As everybody knows, nobody's going to give you a job just because you call and introduce yourself. The idea is to glean information from your contact on the opportunities in the industry and further contacts that could develop into leads.
- You're calling unannounced, so expect any response – from breathtaking rudeness to 'come and see me today'. Practise dealing with various reactions in advance by asking a buddy to do some role-play exercises.
- Try to make sure you sound happy and relaxed – people can 'hear' whether you're down or smiling. You can't always guarantee your mood, of course, but try to keep positive thoughts in mind. Some people even find that putting on a sharp outfit helps boost their confidence.

> **Here's an idea for you...**
>
> Practise your technique by phoning an old friend you haven't spoken to in ages. Prepare as if you were about to cold-call a contact. Let your friend know what you are up to and ask for some feedback on your approach. Try suggesting you should catch up more thoroughly over a meal. That way you can be confident of a warm response, some constructive criticism, plus a good time.

Picking up the phone

You've done the preparation and now you're ready to have a go.

- Begin with people down the bottom of your list and save plum contacts for last. You will get better with practise.
- You probably won't reach your contact the first time. Nevertheless, call them several times before you leave a rehearsed message on their voicemail. Your contact probably isn't all that keen on talking to strangers either and so might put off calling you back.
- Be realistic. When you first try to contact someone new, you'll almost always come across an objection. They might say: 'I'm really busy at the moment.' Try a reply like: 'I realise how busy you must be, but when would it be more convenient to talk?'
- Maintain a courteous stance no matter how disagreeable someone is with you. Getting huffy won't help.
- Talking face to face is the best way to get contacts to open up. Once you've reached a promising contact try to arrange a brief appointment.
- Keep notes that will help you build a relationship with your contact, like their spouse's name, former employers and mutual acquaintances.

Following your call

Once you hang up, confirm in writing the next steps you agreed, like an appointment. After a meeting, always follow up with a thank-you note or email (even if they haven't been much help). Send a brief contact report listing agreed actions.

> *Most of the important things in the world have been accomplished by people who have kept on trying when there seemed to be no hope at all.* Dale Carnegie, American author and motivational speaker

How did it go?

Q. Every time I call they put me through to voicemail or an assistant. Can you help?

A. You just have to have plenty of patience and persevere. If it's a professional organisation, you'll eventually get hold of the person you want to speak to. Then it's a case of getting them to agree a convenient time to call for a fuller chat. Most people will suggest a time if only to get rid of you. Always call at the agreed time and politely pursue your agenda. Remember, you're aiming ideally for a brief face-to-face discussion where you can explain your plans and ask for advice on how to achieve them.

Q. My contact says: 'I can't help you as I'm in a different field'. What do I do?

A. You could try replying something like this: 'I realise we're in different fields but I think my skills apply to your sector too and I wanted to pick your brains about it.'

Q. In spite of using my best opening lines, people sense that I'm really looking for a job and just ask me to send in a CV. How should I combat that?

A. Stick to your guns. Say that you'd be happy to send a CV for a specific position, but that the reason for your call is not to ask for a job but to pick your contact's brains a bit more generally about the way the sector is developing and what opportunities this might present.

16. Be a superstar in cyberspace

A presence on career and social networking sites certainly can help raise your profile. Here's how to determine which ones are worth joining.

Companies spend millions analysing customers' online activity and collecting information about them. Put the boot on the other foot and take control of your own online presence.

Now anyone can find an audience on the internet. Fast broadband connections mean everyone can see anything you choose to post: words, pictures, videos and music. Potentially you can connect with millions via your social networking site profile.

In theory, the web's reach means that a single individual with a laptop can start a worldwide rumour mill or kick-start a trend. But you won't succeed, of course, unless you gain your audience's attention. That's the commodity in shortest supply in the online world and there are already more than 100 million bloggers on the World Wide Web.

Networking

Here's an idea for you...

Build your brand online and offline, simultaneously. Simply building it online is tempting but not enough. You have to work at your personal advancement. Some people write up their own glowing profile on a social networking site then make the mistake of actually believing it. For every hour you spend updating your online profile, spend another in the real world, too. For instance, phone to pitch an idea to a client or suggest a meeting with networking buddies.

Lots of celebrities already demand attention by shrieking 'me, me, me' online as loudly as possible. Wannabe web celebs have to work at it.

Amanda Congdon was once a struggling actress seeking an escape from bit parts and waitressing. She now presents a video blog for American media giant ABC News. She set out to find an outlet for her acting ambitions and got her start fronting a video blog on Craigslist, the internet small ads site. Then she launched her own blog, AmandaAcrossAmerica.com, featuring her interviews with other bloggers and web geeks that she encountered travelling throughout the United States. Her show attracts an audience large enough to propel it into the top 400 or so video blogs.

Amanda has planted herself firmly in the sweet spot between mainstream and new media, a rapidly shrinking space. However, for every one that achieves their ambition, millions don't.

Control your own content

What the web offers you with greater certainty is the ability to control your own content on the new media. Your first step in this direction is to understand the technology.

Idea 16 – **Be a superstar in cyberspace**

When search engines like Google return results, the sites they list are essentially those that score the highest number of links from other sites. You achieve top billing – apart from the paid-for adverts – if your site has more sites linking to it than any other. It's very similar on social networking sites. Your ranking, and visibility, depends on acquiring the most 'friends', rather than links.

Until the search engines change their algorithms (the mathematical routines that calculate the rankings), the top spot is open to web celebs that know how to work the system.

For example, 'google' the name 'Robert' and the top name on the list is not Robert De Niro or Robert Redford but Robert Scoble, an American blogger with search engine and self-promotion expertise. Scoble a self-confessed technology geek, used to be the 'Microsoft Blogger' when he worked for the company. He now produces the Scoble Show, his own video blog, featuring interviews with assorted geeks and internet entrepreneurs. The links from their sites help boost Scoble's web presence.

Manage your digital presence

There are numerous web-based services that can help you control your online presence. If you sign up with ClaimID, their clever software bundles together all the information that you want others to find and makes sure it turns up in a web search when someone enters your name in a search engine.

Others rate your digital presence in terms of how popular and active you are online. One innovative web developer called Garlik has a status monitoring service called QDOS that uses a scoring method based on how many websites carry information about you and how many people visit the site to view the data.

Services like these can help you manage your online reputation. This could be very useful when a recruiter uses a web search to screen candidates for a job in your sector, say; or when a would-be dater scours the web to find mates of their choice.

> Science and technology multiply around us. To an increasing extent they dictate the languages in which we speak and think. Either we use those languages, or we remain mute. J. G. Ballard, British science fiction writer

Idea 16 – **Be a superstar in cyberspace**

How did it go?

Q. I'm updating my Facebook profile and would like to post pictures that show myself off to best advantage for a recruiter. How do I get a picture that helps me get an interview?

A. Look lively – employers generally look for a positive 'can-do' attitude as well as any specific sector knowledge or skills. So forget looking moody and magnificent. A beaming smile does wonders. Get a friend to take loads of shots of you at your most natural; the best professionals always reckon that you look best in a photo when you're relaxed and animated. Enhance your facial tone by wearing a top with a solid bright hue as dark colours can be draining.

Q. I'm an enthusiastic blogger but regularly seem to run out of ideas. What's the secret of a successful blog?

A. Be brilliant and lucky. There are more than 100 million bloggers on the World Wide Web, some supported by fairly sizeable corporate resources. So you really have to have something exceptional to say to attract notice – and you have to be able to sustain it to keep them coming back for more. A tip: the blogosphere shows signs of rivalling traditional news media as the voice of public opinion, particularly for anti-establishment views. Focus on what really matters to you and your passion may just strike a chord with others; provoke enough people to respond and you may kick off a daily interactive rant.

Networking

17. Wear the right clothes

It's not fair but we all judge others by their appearance. Look the part and blend in with people you want to impress using our top tips.

Once upon a time everyone simply put on a suit and they knew they were correctly dressed for most occasions — well not any more. So just what do you wear for business these days?

You're about to meet a chief executive for the first time. Before you have a complete panic over your wardrobe, slow down and breathe deeply. We've all got some common sense so let's use it. First off, what line of business is he or she in?

The realm of the suit
The computer industry and the internet may have revolutionised some people's wardrobes but when it comes to financial institutions, legal firms and accountants it's pretty obvious that a strictly traditional dress code still prevails. Both men and women tend to wear black, navy or grey tailored suits with conservative shirts or tops. Sober ties for men and low-key accessories for women are still the order of the day. On a business visit to a firm in these industries, men

Here's an idea for you...

If you're visiting clients all afternoon and there's no time to change before an evening event make sure you pick an outfit that will run the gamut of all your activities. Wrap dresses are good, as are black single-breasted suits in crepe or lightweight wool. Pair your suit with a top with a slight sheen or crisp solid-coloured shirt. Bring some accessories like flashy jewellery or those killer-heeled sandals to slip on and help transform your outfit from day to night. Some deodorant wipes are useful so you can freshen up quickly before the event.

should stick to a dark suit and tie; women should avoid vibrant or high-fashion outfits that make them stand out from the crowd too much.

In other fields, like headhunting, public relations and management consultancy, there's slightly more flexibility when it comes to office wear. Think of open-necked shirts with sharp suits or cashmere roll-necks paired with simple flared skirts. The look is quite dressy but stylish and contemporary; it's the business image most people currently aspire to today.

Smart casual

On the other end of the spectrum, designers, media moguls and computer entrepreneurs are legendarily casual. However, that doesn't mean they aren't interested in clothes. As a rule, people in the creative industries are the first to pick up on fashion trends. Work outfits can vary from cult jeans with old school trainers to Miu Miu dresses or vintage Ossie Clark. Because the look is so eclectic it's really easy to miss the mark and end up looking like a dork. So, you are better off wearing an outfit that makes you feel comfortable when you do business with creative types – if that's a suit, so be it. Being yourself will win their respect. What they won't tolerate is phoney wannabes.

Evening wear

Nobody looks more sheepish than a man in checked flannel among a sea of penguins. If you have been invited to an evening event and the dress code says

Idea 17 – **Wear the right clothes**

black tie then you must wear it. Men who attend more than three black tie events per year should seriously consider investing in a dinner suit. Hired kit rarely looks or fits right. Women should remember that less is more. You're there on business not to accept an Oscar. So forget the grand entrance in miles of chiffon, leave the tiara at home and no disco diva make-up, please.

We all want to look appropriate when we're meeting someone important. So if you're still feeling unsure after all this advice why not speak to a friend who works in the same industry or – better still – the chief executive's personal assistant and ask for a few tips on what pleases the boss.

Image consultants
Long-term stylists and their magic makeovers aren't just for Hollywood stars any more. All sorts of people, from teachers to bankers, are now employing them. So, if you feel your look is not quite right it might be a good idea to talk to an image consultant. They will show you why one outfit works and another doesn't. This is basic but empowering stuff. It will improve the way you come across to others because you know you'll be looking your best. Investing in this kind of help will cost you, obviously, but it can enhance your visibility and transform your career.

Because in fashion, as in life, context is everything, you must dress for the place you're in: professionally, emotionally and physically. Vanessa Friedman, *Financial Times*

How did it go?

Q. What do I do if I am dressed up and they're not?
A. First off, thank your lucky stars you are overdressed rather than underdressed, which is near impossible to handle. If you can, discreetly, make yourself look and feel more comfortable by loosening your tie or removing your jacket. Then try to relax: most people secretly find it flattering that you made all that effort for them.

Q. The smell of my favourite cologne makes my spirits soar. Should I spritz myself with it before an important meeting?
A. Calvin Klein's *Obsession* or Dior's *Tendre Poison* might be your favourite cologne but that doesn't mean the fragrance appeals to everyone – not to mention that colognes can trigger allergies and asthma attacks for some people. So, if you're visiting unfamiliar turf, go easy on the cologne or – safer yet – skip it altogether.

Q. Help! I just noticed a stain on my shirt and I am about to give a talk. What can I do?
A. Assess the damage – will the stain come out with a little soap and water? If not go out and buy a new one if there is enough time. Otherwise is there someone in the office who keeps a spare shirt in their desk drawer for just such emergencies or can you persuade a colleague to do you a favour and exchange shirts? If there's no option but to go ahead – stain and all – acknowledge what's obvious by turning it into a joke.

18. Mind your manners

Basic courtesy makes a big difference when you're trying to network and build relationships.

Today's business environment is very fast paced. With less and less time available for face-to-face interaction, it is more important than ever to mind your manners.

Grace us with your presence
Chronic lateness and casual timekeeping are very inconsiderate. Don't waste others' time waiting for you. Arriving at an event once it's started makes it more difficult to break into the swing of things. Phoning at the last minute to cancel a meeting isn't a popular move either. An unexplained 'no show' is downright insulting. If your job takes you out of the office for part of the day, tell those back at the ranch where you are and when you'll be back. Struggling in to work when you're sick can score you points with your colleagues if there's a deadline to meet but probably not if you're ill with something contagious. On the same note, don't leave your co-workers in the lurch if you pull a 'sickie' (i.e. choose a day that's the least inconvenient).

Watch your words
Most of us can't help occasionally letting out the odd profanity or two in the office. But, according to a recent survey, nine out of ten employers say swearing

> **Here's an idea for you...**
>
> Before you fire off an angry retort to that offensive email you just received stop and think awhile. Read it over again. Show it to a close friend or work buddy if you need a second opinion. Did the sender really mean to be so abrupt or were they just being hasty and sloppy? Once you've calmed down compose and send a polite, dignified reply.

in the workplace creates a lasting bad impression and definitely affects their opinion of an employee. So, watch the bad language, especially in front of older colleagues who might take offence, or children for whom you are supposed to be a role model.

Blanking other people
Not greeting people you know with a smile and a hello is plain bad form. You may be tired, in a hurry, incredibly busy; under intense pressure and very stressed, but all of these are poor excuses – and there is never, ever a good reason for rudeness. A few pleasantries go a long way towards getting you to where you want to be.

Responding to emails
Emails are possibly the number one source of offence in the workplace today and most of it is unintended. Be careful what you put in emails. Don't compose them in haste only to repent them later. Ill thought-out words can come across as rude. If you're up against a tight deadline a quick holding message – just a couple of lines – should do the trick. Then get back to the sender in more detail when you have more time. Don't send chain emails or joke emails. It just doesn't look productive. Avoid sending fat files that clog up the recipient's inbox without asking for permission first. Don't send circulars to everyone in your address book or company-wide emails, except in very specific circumstances. They are so impersonal and usually ineffective.

Idea 18 – **Mind your manners**

The mobile turn-off

It is rude to answer your mobile during a meeting; the same goes for checking for new messages or texts. Switch it off – your colleagues deserve your undivided attention. Also, respect confidentiality when answering your mobile in public: speak quietly and cautiously – for example, stick to first names, only. Otherwise you or your caller could inadvertently reveal sensitive information and you never know who might be listening.

A proper introduction

Okay, you're nervous and the outcome of this meeting is critical. That makes it doubly important that everybody knows each other before getting down to the matter at hand. Not only is skipping the introductions very impolite but it also makes it awkward for others to have a conversation with one another. The client is the most important person in the room; without them you have no business. Always address them first and introduce them to the rest of your colleagues. If your host forgets to introduce you to others in the group, be sure to save face for them and introduce yourself; make your relationship to the host clear in your introduction.

Manners are an essential part of the image you project at work.

Paul Jacobs, Managing Director of Office Angels

How did it go?

Q. When I go to meetings, I get really confused about when to stand and when to remain seated. Any tips?

A. Traditionally, women remain seated whenever someone enters a room and men stand. Today both sexes should rise to greet visitors as a mark of respect, especially in a business situation. Unless they are frequent visitors, you should always greet clients at reception or the office entrance and lead them to and from the meeting room.

Q. One of my colleagues had a drink too many at a wine bar after work and said some things she shouldn't have to a workmate. How does she begin to make amends?

A. She's got a lot of lost ground to make up. Hopefully, she's learnt at some cost that an office night out isn't the place to air 'issues'. Offering an explanation or sending a note and flowers can help, but her workmate doesn't have to accept her apology. Some mature reflection on her thoughtless behaviour and lack of consideration for someone's feelings will eventually lessen her embarrassment.

Q. My client – otherwise a lovely guy – makes the occasional sexist gaffe. Do I just ignore him or say something?

A. In general it's wise to make some allowances for age and background before reacting to such remarks. It is perfectly okay to keep on pretending you haven't heard his more extreme opinions. It is also fine to make a witty quip if you feel he's being insulting. Humour is far less confrontational than a sermonising speech about his inappropriate talk but still gets your message across.

19. A little flattery gets you everywhere

Brush up those interpersonal skills, like managing insecure people and defusing aggression.

Hit the right buttons and the object of your charm offensive will become easier to deal with. The result: a better chance of engaging their support.

Most of us respond well to a little social stroking, especially when things are not going so well in our lives. This applies to even the most confident and glamorous looking people, who are often the most insecure (they have developed a confident manner to paper over their feelings of insecurity).

Show people lots of appreciation when they please you and praise them for a job well done. Take a tip from generations of school and college students who have learnt to score high marks for classroom participation by adopting the mantra 'nod, smile and take notes' whenever their teachers look at them.

Teachers – and the rest of us – like to feel recognised. It spurs us on to even greater efforts. After all, it's satisfying to feel you do your job well; it's also motivating to know how what you are doing fits into the general scheme of things.

Learn to give, and take, compliments. There are usually plenty of people who feel they have a right to criticise you at work and/or at home (either that or I'm being picked on!), so make the most of a compliment – accept it graciously.

Lay it on

If you learn to use it well, flattery can be a useful tool in getting the best out of people who are in a position to help your ambitions. The most successful flatterers always focus on a genuine quality possessed by the object of their attention (e.g. intelligence, good looks or a sense of humour). There has to be some grain of truth in a compliment, enough for the receiver to recognise the quality in themselves.

Defuse conflict gently

It's almost always best to deal with aggressive behaviour face to face rather than by email or voice message. The exception is if you judge you're in danger of someone actually throwing a punch at you – in which case you'd do better to take evasive action.

Try to defuse the situation by getting the irate person to realise how badly they are behaving. Echo their complaint or accusation back at them, prefaced with a line such as 'You're saying that …' followed by their very own words.

That shows that you have listened to them and understood what they are saying. It also keeps you both focused on the issue – which helps prevent it escalating into a wider argument. In a heated exchange, look around for support from colleagues and try to bring them in, whatever side they are on. The chances are

Idea 19 – **A little flattery gets you everywhere**

that the irate person will simmer down when they realise that they are a) behaving badly, b) not isolated, and c) possibly outnumbered. Then, see if you can reach a satisfactory outcome, including, if necessary, an agreement to disagree.

Dealing with an angry boss

If your boss is habitually angry, special rules apply, since you could be looking for a new job if you don't handle the situation. Inside every poor manager is a quiet voice saying 'you are a poor manager'. Insecure bosses often compensate by becoming arrogant and aggressive; they shout and scream to try to get their own way. The key is to be diplomatic and allow them to feel in control. Let them rant – it will probably last no more than a few minutes. Do not join in under any circumstances, as they are just looking for any sign of opposition to crush.

> **Here's an idea for you…**
>
> If you have a boss that takes credit for your ideas, get your retaliation in first. Let others know about your bright ideas, especially senior management. Put your name on the cover of your proposals to make sure your prior claim is documented. Then, if your idea turns out to be a winner, tell your boss's boss how grateful you were for your boss's encouragement – even if they haven't helped at all. This avoids annoying your boss and makes you look like a star team player.

The secret is to make yourself scarce until your boss has cooled off. Insist that 'we need to handle this rationally' and say you will come back later when 'we can look at this again'. Then whatever your boss says, leave. Stay calm and you will succeed in handling things on your own terms.

What valour cannot win, flattery may.
Publius Syrus, writer of maxims in Ancient Rome

How did it go?

Q. I'm nervous about making a presentation to an important client. A female colleague who knows him of old laughs and says 'just wear your leather skirt and you'll be fine'. Isn't that a bit low?

A. It's a fact of life that a little seduction can work wonders with some people – mainly men, it has to be said. However, those who employ these charms must tread very carefully. You might find you've gained a bad reputation or, worse, are on the receiving end of harassment. There's no harm in following your colleague's advice and wearing the skirt guaranteed to please providing your presentation and behaviour is utterly professional.

Q. My boss overheard me sounding off to a colleague about work, including some unflattering comments about his abilities. How can I put myself back in his good books?

A. It's never a good idea to bitch about colleagues or managers at work because it usually gets back to them. If you have issues with someone's attitude, it's better to take them aside for a frank discussion. In this case you're probably into damage limitation – your concern is with your boss's ability, something he can't do much about. He may wonder what else you are keeping from him. Find a suitable occasion to talk openly about the problem; at least he may be reassured that you are not completely two-faced. However, it might take some time and conspicuous effort for you to restore the previous confidence he had in you.

20. Good vibrations

From flirting to making new business contacts, your body language says so much about you. Understanding what your body is expressing will help you come across in an open and relaxed way.

When you're networking you want to establish an easy intimacy with your peers and build relationships of trust, so it helps if you seem warm and easily understood.

Only 7% of the impact of any message is verbal; 38% is tone of voice; and a staggering 55% is non-verbal. Like any language, the more fluent you are, the easier it is to communicate with others. So, don't try too hard. There's actually nothing better than being with a person who is at ease with themselves. Greeting new contacts with a smile and a firm handshake can go a long way to starting a good relationship. Smiling is infectious – people can even 'hear' you smile on the phone.

If you're having to try too hard, it probably means you aren't getting along with the person you are with, so move on to where you're appreciated and can be yourself. However, some situations you can't avoid. Speaking in public or making a presentation at work are two of the things that most people dread. That anxiety interferes with your natural rhythm and freedom of expression.

Recognise your body-language habits

Folding your arms is the most obvious way of announcing that you want to protect yourself from what's going on around you. Most of us acquire other common little habits – called displacement activities – that give away our inner conflict. These include:

- biting your fingernails or playing with your hair,
- clasping your hands in front or behind you, or putting them in your pockets,
- clutching papers or books to your chest,
- fiddling with your clothes (e.g. tugging at the hem of your top to pull it down over your waist),
- taking shallow breaths, especially when you're about to say something,
- shifting your weight from one foot to the other.

Holding on to tension can become a habit, tightening your stomach and restricting your breathing. This is what interrupts your natural flow and can make your voice sound thin or whiney. What you're doing is trying to make yourself smaller, a sure sign that you don't really want to be doing what you're doing. The secret, of course, is to actually want to be right there doing what you're doing, in the knowledge that everything will probably be fine. The experts call it being 'present'. It's that state that great athletes and actors get into when they perform at their best. Babies and toddlers live almost constantly in the present, so you can't say you don't know what it's like!

The body says what words cannot.
Martha Graham, modern dance pioneer

Stay connected

The easiest way to stay connected is to look and listen to the other people there. Mirror what they're doing: take a lead from their body language and reflect it in the way that you sit, stand or talk. Play your part in the group: respond to what other people say and how they say it; pick up on a comment that someone else has made when it comes to your turn to speak.

Instant calmer

For instant calm in a stressful situation like preparing for an interview or a presentation, try this advice from Patsy Rodenburg, Head of the Voice Department at Britain's National Theatre: 'Connect with the floor and push down on your feet to make you feel stronger, then think about moving forward a tiny bit on the balls of your feet. If you're sitting down in a meeting and feel anxious, then lean forward for a moment, your elbows on your knees and take a couple of breaths. You can ease the tension and no one will know you're doing it.'

Occupy space

The best general direction in this context is to 'occupy space', meaning that you don't think about your nerves but focus largely on your external surroundings – including the people around you. This can be particularly important for women, who, according to research using hidden cameras in offices, are more likely than their male counterparts to make themselves smaller by folding their arms or clutching papers to their chests. The stereotype male, on the other hand, tosses papers all over his desk and waves his arms about expansively to help make a point.

Here's an idea for you...

Dig out an old photograph of yourself at two or three years old. Look at how sturdy and robust you are and how you look ready for anything that excites your curiosity. Use the picture to remind yourself of what's beneath your complex adult make-up: the poise and posture to take on any activity as long as you learn to release yourself from your acquired habits of holding on to tension.

# How did it go?

Q. *How do I know which displacement activities I have when I can't see myself displaying them in a pressure situation?*
A. Have a quiet word with your friends on a suitable occasion and simply ask them what distinctive habits they notice about you. In my case, apparently, it's a certain way of chewing my jaw when I'm nervous – a bit like a sheep eats. They'll probably tell you they find some of these annoying but others are endearing and help make you the person they know and love, so don't try to eradicate them; just use them to notice when you are tense or nervous and need to relax.

Q. *When I'm at a networking event, how can I tell whether I can join in with a group that's already talking together from their body language?*
A. You can usually see it in their eyes. If they're willing to make eye contact with you, it's probable that they would welcome another person joining them. If not, they are probably engaged in a private conversation, so move on to another group.

Idea 20 – **Good vibrations**

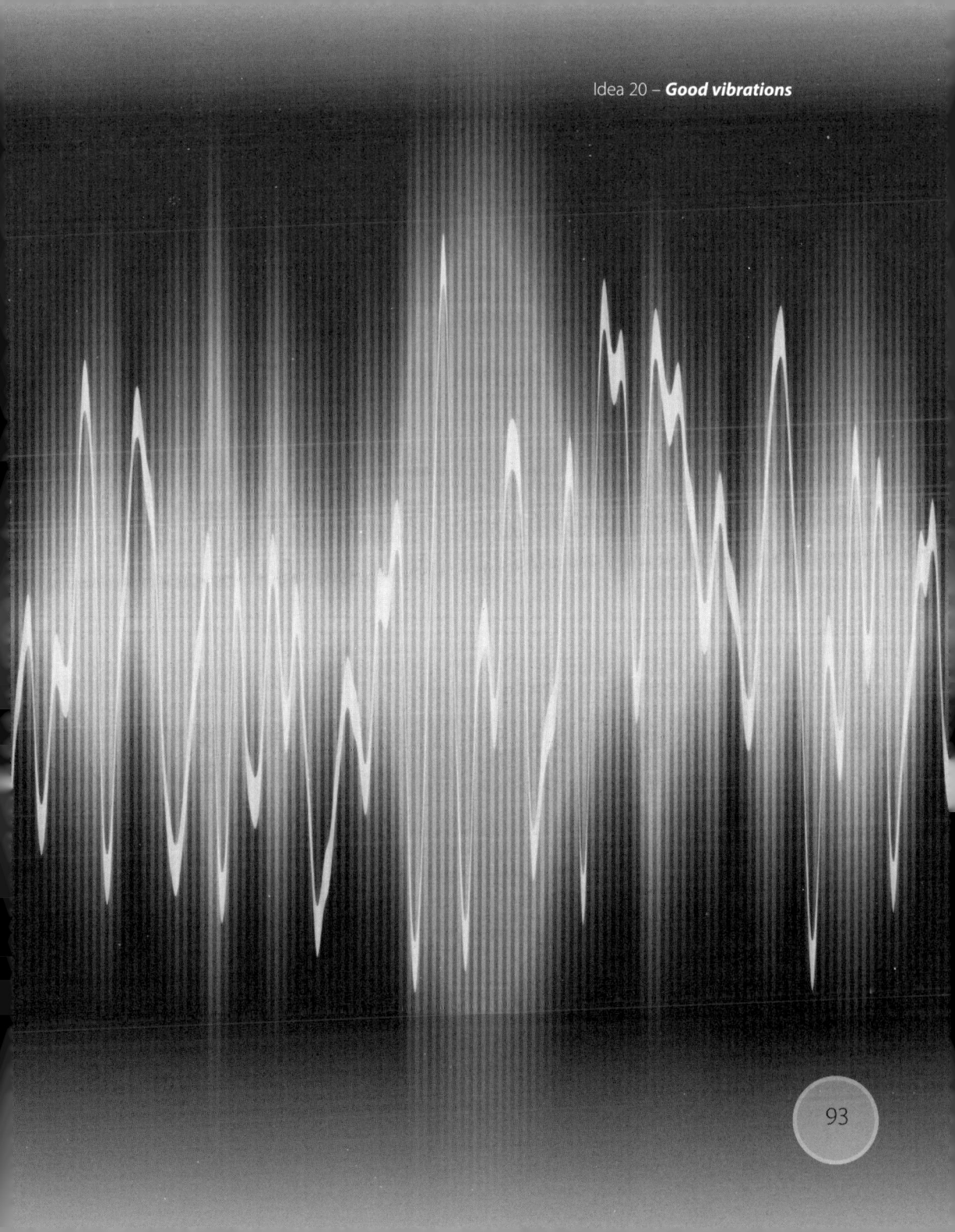

21. Flex that Rolodex

Whether you use traditional index cards or a brand new software package, it's important to keep track of your contact's details.

Who doesn't appreciate it when an acquaintance remembers your wife's name and enquires after her? Personal touches make a big difference when you're trying to build relationships, which is why it's vital to make notes on who you meet and what they say.

Most people would agree Bill Clinton has got consummate social skills and is a first-class networker. What's less well known about him is that all that seemingly effortless charm is made possible thanks to his inveterate note-taking. Since his early days at college when he first decided on a political career, Clinton has been recording information on anyone he came across, from acquaintances and classmates to political advisers and his professors, who might prove helpful in the future.

Clinton's cards

He would write their contact details on an index card, including a few lines on where they met and any relevant information he gleaned from them. Originally, Clinton kept his annotated cards in alphabetical order in cardboard boxes. Any subsequent interchanges or meetings were jotted down. When he sent out campaign or fund-raising letters to contacts, he and his aides would record the date and responses. By the time all these files were computerised in the early 1980s, he had assembled over 10,000 names. This immensely valuable database helped get him elected when he eventually ran for president in the 1990s.

As Clinton once told a *New York Times* reporter, he still continues to record information on contacts each and every day. One of his final tasks most evenings is to make notes on those handy index cards about the people he met that day.

Like so many things that are good for you, such as regular exercise, making notes after a meeting can be tedious and time consuming. Of course, it is much easier to simply file a contact's business card for future reference and count on remembering their details. But odds are, your memory will let you down – there's no pay-off without hard work. So, even if you have only a tiny fraction of Clinton's discipline and drive, recording information on your contacts is a good habit to get into.

> Here's an idea for you...
> If you have trouble remembering people's names – let alone their anniversaries – practise using a handy memory prompt. For example, associate the person's name with an animal whose name begins with the same letter, such as antelope for Alice. Visualise distinguishing characteristics such as a moustache, funky glasses or long black hair so you can use them as prompts at a later date. It also helps you remember someone's name if you repeat it aloud when you're first introduced and use it several times during the course of your first conversation.

What to record
Apart from the obvious telephone number and address, the sort of things you need to record are meeting dates and places, introductions made and useful information your contacts gave you that day. Note down snippets of their career history such as former employers and remember to jot down any mutual acquaintances. As you get to know them better you might want to include more personal information, like hobbies, things they collect or sports they play. Once

you begin seeing people on a regular basis, it's a good idea to jot down their birthday, the dates of big anniversaries and key facts about their home life, like their kids' names, spouses' professions, even what pets they have.

There is no need to make very lengthy or detailed notes. They are meant to be a quick reference, a memory cue you can turn to before a phone call, a meeting or an appointment.

Where to record it
Though techno wizards might record and store their contact data on contact management programs such as ACT, Maximizer or Goldmine, many people still prefer to hand write their notes. As a result, the Rolodex, with its retro good looks and old-fashioned practicality, has enjoyed a resurgence in popularity in recent years. Personally, I tend to jot down most of this type of information in my address book but that can get a little messy. I also have colleagues with boxes full of index cards just like Bill Clinton.

> *You can make more friends in two months by becoming interested in other people than you can in two years by trying to get other people interested in you.*

Dale Carnegie, American author and motivational speaker

How did it go?

Q. A workmate suggested we pool information on contacts so we can both generate more business. Doesn't that sound like a great idea?

A. This might seem like a fabulous opportunity, but avoid it like the plague. Putting a friend in touch with a contact is one thing; sharing large amounts of other people's personal information is quite another. For a start, it's illegal without their permission, and rightly so. Put yourself in your contact's shoes: how would you feel if a complete stranger knew facts about your family, like the names of your children or that your spouse is a senior partner at a hot city firm?

Q. I haven't seen some old colleagues in five or six years. Is it time to remove their details from my files?

A. It is never a good idea to delete contacts' details, even if you haven't spoken to them in ages. You never know when that information might come in handy and your shared history will help you to reconnect quickly. Of course, your notes will become out of date if you do not keep up with your contacts. Since you last spoke, they may have changed employers, remarried or now have three kids instead of two. Nevertheless, the core of what you had in common will remain the same.

22. Darling, you shouldn't have!

Gift giving is a minefield. Nevertheless, the appropriate present at the right time can cement relationships and help build a resilient network of contacts.

Everyone likes to feel appreciated. From a $20,000 goody-bag to an invitation to an event or the promise of a hot tip, gifts can help build relationships.

Give to get

It may seem mercenary, but you usually have to spend before you receive. Giving doesn't necessarily have to cost a lot – although, let's face it, money helps – but it does take effort and imagination. For example, making sure your chosen contacts are the first to hear news of a special promotion or price discount that your company is about to offer gives them the message that you're treating them specially.

Don't underestimate sheer childish greed. Few of us ever grow out of the thrill of free stuff. The goody-bag is just as popular at business events as kids' parties and is positively *de rigueur* at fashion shows and celebrity bashes. Few celebs leave a Hollywood party without one – which might contain designer clothes, jewellery and technology gizmos worth $20,000 or more – and some have been known to pocket two or more.

Spark their imagination

Get to know your contacts' personal interests outside work and pander to them shamelessly. One of the most cost-effective gifts is a magazine subscription: every issue that hits their desk or, better still, pops through their letter-box reminds them who was thoughtful enough to order it.

Choose a gift that's appropriate: not too cheap ('is that all they think of me?') and not too pricey ('what are they after?'). Choosing a gift that can be used when and where the recipient likes shows respect for someone's busy schedule (e.g. a voucher for a weekend stay in a hotel; make that a stay for two and you show that you understand the recipient is so much in demand that they value some quality time with their spouse).

Target your gifts

Treat special contacts extra well – for example, buyers who can place a direct order for your goods or services. Media people who can offer (or deny) good editorial coverage in their magazines deserve extra special attention. One junior manager at a fashion retailer made it her business to deal with editorial contacts at fashion magazines. She would contact them with news about new clothing ranges or fragrances her company was stocking. She would give them the news about sales and discounts on a particular range so they could take advantage of offers first. This made business sense for her company but it also led in time to her being offered a career move to a famous magazine, the 'bible' of the rag trade.

> **Here's an idea for you...**
>
> Search for a way to have a hand in organising special events at your company, from corporate hospitality to discounts and promotions. Make an effort to find out about them and put yourself in a position to bring news of offers to clients. Then, when there's a difficult decision about who to invite, you might be able to tip the balance in favour of your contacts, who may reward your efforts. They'll thank you for it and remember you when there's a favour on offer at their end.

Always say 'thank you'

Gift givers will not forget if you fail to show appreciation for something that they've done for you. For example, when a well-known clothing retailer hosted a fashion show for a magazine at their flagship store, a member of the editorial team sent a wonderful bunch of flowers to say thank you. Unfortunately, the company director failed to send a thank-you note back. The retailer's name was consequently out of favour within the editorial office and for 3 years they barely won a mention in the columns of the hallowed fashion journal.

Tip like a toff

In lots of jobs, from the car jockey to the hairdresser and even the nurse at the health clinic, people depend on the tips they receive to make ends meet. So, however poor you may be feeling yourself, always tip generously. Be aware of local differences in expectation: 10–15% is the norm in Europe; 15–20% in North America. Many businesses fail to pass on gratuities paid by credit card to their staff at all; or in full – some deduct the tax they have to pay on gratuities before distributing the remainder. Paying tips in cash avoids this.

Gifts are a way of establishing bonds of mutual care and obligation.

Marcel Mauss, French ethnographer, *Essai sur le don*, 1925

Idea 22 – **Darling, you shouldn't have!**

How did it go?

Q. I seem to keep giving without receiving much back in return. Any suggestions?

A. You can't expect immediate results but you should certainly keep track of the results of gift giving. You need to know who shows appreciation of your thoughtfulness and what difference it makes so you can focus on what delivers the best results. For example, always make a note of who attends events that you organise – and who sent a thank-you note – so you can review your guest list for the next time.

Q. Should I even give something I can't bear to part with?

A. Let's say you can get your hands on hard-to-obtain tickets for a hit show. Yes, it'll take a considerable effort of will to pass up the chance to see the show yourself and deliver the surprise with a throwaway line like 'I've got some tickets I can't use' but you can bet your contact will appreciate the gesture all the more and think most highly of you.

Q. What kind of gifts can I give safely when I don't know much about the recipient's preferences?

A. There's a useful trend towards showing restraint that you could adopt. For example, giving gifts that mix gratitude with social responsibility, such as environmentally friendly spa products or an invitation to an exciting charity auction that raises funds for a good cause. At the top of the cost range, a ticket to the opera may be expensive but is seen to support a cultural activity and so scores bonus points.

23. The nepotism card

Your family and their friends can open new doors and help smooth your path.

In today's competitive job market it is important to use every advantage. Don't hesitate to ask your parents for assistance in achieving your dream.

When you were growing up, you heard your parents discuss what they had done that day around the dinner table – possibly in great detail. Whether they were farmers or lawyers or owned a corner shop, you picked up on their experience and their moods. Their conversations exposed you to the highs of their working lives, like closing an important deal, and the lows, such as how hard it is to make money during an economic downturn. When they were successful, they passed on their enthusiasm. When they struggled, you learnt that it was possible to cope with difficulties.

You picked up on how passionate they were about the way they made their living. That made it seem natural to you, too. You couldn't wait to follow in their footsteps.

Parental role models
A successful parent can be an inspiring role model. But it can also seem like a distinct handicap. People will inevitably compare you with your parents and their

high expectations can be a bit daunting. You worry you'll never be as successful as your mother or father. On the other hand, if your own career takes off meteorically, people will assume it's been handed to you on a plate just because of your parent's professional renown and connections. That can drive you to work twice as hard to prove your worth and assert your own identity.

Stella McCartney would be the first to admit that she leveraged her famous father's name to launch her career and plundered the family address book, a veritable 'who's who', for contacts. But she chose her own path and has established an international reputation in her own field as a fashion designer.

It's all relative

For all the potency of its past association with unfair advantage and unjustified preferment, nowadays nepotism has its limits. In today's highly competitive world, it's rare for anybody to be able to shoehorn a relative into a plum job just because of their family connection.

Let's say you want to be an actor, just like your mother. She might be able to introduce you to an influential director or ensure you get an audition. But she won't be able to guarantee you get the part. Any sustained success is down to your own effort and ability. Nepotism might give you an entrée but if you're not actually gifted and hard working, you won't go very far.

> *Here's an idea for you...*
>
> Gain knowledge from other families' experiences. A number of networking groups such as the *Family Business Network* and the *Institute for Family Business* now exist specifically to provide mutual support for family-run firms. They encourage you and your relatives to develop a peer-to-peer relationship with members of other family businesses and to share distinct concerns such as how to prepare the next generation for leadership and to learn from each other.

Parents these days are less inclined to push their children into the family business or a 'good, steady job'. They know their efforts may be counter-productive, given the contrariness of their offspring and the choices open to them. They are more likely to see what their children want to do and to encourage their ambition. Yet recent research tells us that 10% of university graduates still choose to go into the same field as their father and this figure rises to nearly 20% in some professions, like medicine and health care.

A new chip off the block

Of course you could grow up deciding that you want do something completely different from your parents. But even so you can more than likely still get them to open doors for you and take advantage of their connections.

Say you have decided to carve out a career in interior design and your father is in the property business. Take him up on his offer to introduce you to new prospects. Perhaps he needs some help dressing show homes or maybe he has clients who need some advice on how to decorate their new homes.

Even if your parents can't help you with contacts in your preferred profession, they may still have done their bit for your career. Where else did you acquire those first-class networking skills other than around the family table?

> *There is nothing wrong with nepotism, as long as you keep it in the family.* Barry Norman, British film critic

Idea 23– **The nepotism card**

How did it go?

Q. I'm a newspaper editor. My nephew – a journalism student – wants me to put him forward for an internship. I'd like to help but I don't want to be accused of favouritism. What do you suggest?

A. Did you know the word nepotism derives from the Latin *nepos* meaning nephew? During the fourteenth century, Italians started using the term *nepotismo* to describe the papal practice of giving their sons – dubbed 'nephews' to disguise their illegitimacy – all the best appointments. However, you are not a Renaissance Pope. So, feel free to help your nephew apply but defend yourself against accusations about special treatment. Ultimately it will be talent and determination that wins him the internship.

Q. My sister and I work at my family's catering company. We have always been competitive but recently things have turned nasty. I don't want to fall out completely. Any advice?

A. You're right to be worried. Sibling rivalry won't just ruin your relationship, it can undermine or even destroy your family's business. It's time you both remembered that when a family runs a business together the success of that firm comes first. Your individual rights and entitlements come second. Focus on working as a team and creating a unified vision. What will help is if you try to see things from each other's perspective. If communication has broken down, consider hiring a consultant to mediate a workable solution.

24. Accentuate the positive

Like it or not, your reputation goes before you, so you should do whatever you can to make it work positively for you.

You may think your reputation can take care of itself, but in today's competitive world, talent and integrity are not enough. You need to give your reputation a helping hand.

Blowing your own trumpet, trying to score brownie points with your boss. It's all a bit beneath you, isn't it? Surely it's unnecessary: talent will always out. Well, not always, unfortunately. Talent might out eventually, but meanwhile people a lot less talented than you might step in and seize that opportunity. Have you noticed, for example, that even quite uncompetitive people no longer take a chance on favourable news about them reaching the right ears. They give their reputation a hand by routinely forwarding complimentary emails from satisfied clients to their bosses. So, put aside your reservations and recognise you are in a competitive market.

Treat others the way you'd like them to treat you
Talking yourself up does not mean you have to compromise on your values. Managing your reputation is not a substitute for talent or integrity. Your

Idea 24 – **Accentuate the positive**

reputation can only build on reality, not replace it. So, the soundest advice is to be the best in your field, always kind to animals and an all-round good egg.

Apart from anything else, most people are good at telling the difference between a manufactured image and reality. For instance, if you're the kind of person that blames everyone but yourself when things don't go according to plan, friends and colleagues will soon notice. Try asking colleagues, for example, if they would want to work with you again on another occasion. Their story is normally surprisingly consistent because everyone notices our very basic human characteristics.

Your technical skills are not enough by themselves. 'People think if they are technically good, that's enough,' says Christiane Wuillamie, a successful business angel and founder of City IT services supplier CWB. 'But it's how you handle people that counts.'

'You get known if you treat people badly,' says Wuillamie. In particular, she says you should never underestimate the importance of any conversation. 'Always be nice to people, even if you think they are junior to you,' she recommends. 'Be civilised. Treat them fairly. People do remember. It always comes back to you.'

Pick your friends and relationships

In spite of increased social mobility and the scope that the internet gives for joining instant communities, people still judge you by the company you keep. So, pick your friends and colleagues carefully.

> **Here's an idea for you...**
>
> Don't ignore the most direct and powerful source of enhancing your reputation: word-of-mouth recommendation from a satisfied customer. The next time you complete a good piece of work for your boss or a client, ask them for a written testimonial or a quote captured on tape that you can place on your website or – better still – play to a prospect during a face-to-face meeting.

Networking

Take a tip from Michael Caine, the famous movie actor. Early in his career he went to Hollywood to make a picture with Shirley Maclaine, who was a big star at the time. He'd yet to make his name in America and found that no one in Hollywood would ever return his calls. But then Maclaine threw a party to welcome him to Hollywood. All the big stars attended – not to meet *him* but because it was *her* party. After that, doors opened and he was on his way.

It's not always the most obvious person – like your boss – who holds the key to your future. If you don't get on well with the gatekeepers, like the boss's secretary, you may find it difficult to arrange meetings with the people that wield the power in an organisation. So try to be nice to everybody. Broaden your range: your boss might feel a bit threatened by someone with talent and ambition but your boss's boss might see your true worth and mention you to colleagues.

Find a fast track for your reputation
Becoming known for one thing has a way of leveraging your reputation at another – think of that colleague who's in training for the Olympic Games or works as a local councillor in their spare time. Try to make time to pursue outside interests that will produce a halo effect. Alternatively, look for an opportunity to take part in industry events or conferences where you can boost your company's reputation and fast track your own.

Regard your good name as the richest jewel you can possibly possess. Socrates

Idea 24 – **Accentuate the positive**

How's it going?

Q. What I do at work is similar to what hundreds of my colleagues do – how can I establish a reputation for myself as an outstanding individual?

A. You can establish a reputation for lots besides expertise in a specific area – e.g. for being ambitious or for having integrity, for always doing what you say you will. In fact, recruitment specialists look out for people who stand out beyond the normal scope of their job descriptions. Give them some evidence of demonstrable qualities, like drive and ambition (e.g. how you have overcome a particularly challenging situation in your personal or social life)

Q. My boss/my client is willing to give me a reference/testimonial but suggests he heads it 'To whom it may concern'. I'd much prefer a personalised letter. What can you suggest?

A. When you're asking for a testimonial or you need a reference from your boss, draft it yourself and ask them to sign it. Submit it clearly marked 'draft', so they have the option to change it. That way you can emphasise the aspects of your recent experience that will help raise your profile in the way that will help you most in your chosen career direction.

Networking

25. There just aren't enough hours in the day

Don't let your busy schedule lead to lost opportunities. Try these quick and effective networking techniques for the time-poor.

You know you should do more networking but deadlines, long hours and your home life seem to get in the way. Here are ways to extract the maximum benefit from what time you do have.

These tips might simply seem like clichés and well-worn maxims but they have all been tried and tested, and they work.

- *Look the part.* If you appear smart and well groomed at work you look organised and people will assume you mean business and take you more seriously. The catch is, with today's relaxed dress code, what does 'smart dress' mean? Have a good look at what the most upwardly mobile people in your business wear and take your cue from them.

- *Make the best use of your time.* Prioritise wisely. Are you making the most of what time you have? For example, do you really need to finish that paperwork this morning when you could be at a networking event instead? Couldn't you order those groceries online rather than visit the supermarket on your way home? Perhaps you could use that time to catch up with a former colleague over drinks. And why not use your travel or commuting time to call those people you met at the conference?

- *Do lots of coffee.* Business lunches are a good way to get to know people and strengthen relationships but by the time you've reached the restaurant and had your meal they do take up a large chunk of a busy day. Why not meet people for coffee or a soft drink, if you prefer, instead. You'll accomplish just as much in far less time.

- *Always carry your business cards.* This applies to everyone, not just the impossibly-stretched-for-time brigade. From dinner parties to airport lounges, you never know who you'll meet; it just might be someone who could help you or that you could help. This is not to suggest you shower your business cards around like confetti. That won't get you anywhere. Rather, give them out selectively to people with whom you really click. Your card will prompt their memory when you follow up.

- *Reconnect with old acquaintances.* You worked together well in the past but you haven't spoken in ages. Neither of you has had a free moment since.

Idea 25 – **There just aren't enough hours in the day**

Nevertheless, you've already bonded and you have good history together. Well, squeeze a space in that hectic schedule of yours and get back in contact. The fact is that it takes less effort to rekindle old relationships than to try to establish a connection with someone new.

- *Remember people's names.* Everyone likes to be acknowledged and recognised. The more you make people feel valued, the more positive will be your impact and influence with them. A quick and effective way to make someone feel special is to commit their name to memory and address them by it whenever you can. It's a surprisingly powerful tool when you're trying to build ties.

- *Listen attentively.* Adept networkers give people their undivided attention when they're talking to them. You won't have to cover the same ground twice if you listen carefully and you'll remember more. Communication goes beyond mere words so take note of their tone, inference and body language too. Ask plenty of questions and don't be afraid to clarify something you didn't understand. Good listeners forge stronger links.

> *Here's an idea for you...*
>
> After a particularly good meeting, rather than following up with the usual impersonal email, why not post a letter instead? These days the postman rarely brings us anything except bills and junk mail. It doesn't take any longer to hand write a thank-you note or card but its impact will be that much greater. Your thoughtful effort will be remembered and will help you to stand out from others.

- *Follow up selectively.* As a rule, only contact people with whom you felt you could do business or had a good rapport. New contacts tend not to respond first time round; they're busy too and they don't know you well enough yet to put you on top of their list. Don't waste time chasing them incessantly. Understand the difference between a lead and a referral. New contacts take time to warm up. If you have been introduced to someone, they know who you are and are expecting to hear from you – make them your number one priority.

> Avoiding the phrase 'I don't have time ...', will soon help you to realise that you do have the time needed for just about anything you choose to accomplish in life.

Bo Bennett, businessman, motivational speaker and author

How did it go?

Q. Normally I am far too busy to attend networking events but this one sounded particularly promising and I've managed to rearrange my diary. How do I make the most of this rare opportunity?

A. Go with a clear idea of how to introduce yourself and your organisation in a concise memorable way. Once you're there don't just spend your time hanging out with individuals you already know well; approach as many new people as possible. Find out their needs and let them get to know you better. The more you interact with others the more likely you are to make a connection to follow up.

Q. I want everyone to know I've just had an article published. In order to save time I plan to tout my success via email. Any thoughts?

A. Congratulations, having an article published is a networking coup. In principle, email is an efficient way to promote it. However, don't just write a generic letter and send it to your entire address book. Bombard people with spam and they'll press the delete button. To produce a more positive response, you must treat your recipients as individuals. That doesn't mean a separate email for each person but you will need to create something personal and engaging. Address the recipient by name – no 'Dear friends', please. Don't waste your own and other people's time. Mail your message appropriately; only share your achievement with people you think it might interest.

26. Make contacts before you're ready for a change

Don't wait until you're looking for the next career move. Take the initiative and establish good relationships at every stage.

Timing is everything. When new opportunities present themselves, make sure you're prepared to hit the ground running.

The perfect job won't be there waiting for you when you decide it's time to make a move. But headhunters looking for candidates will contact you when there's a suitable job if you have an established relationship and you keep them up to date on your progress and availability.

Network, network, network
At times you need your networking buddies to act as cheerleaders, encouraging you from the sidelines when times are tough; at other times, they are a sounding board for your dreams and ambitions. You, of course, have to do the same for them. Then, when a recruiter or headhunter looking for candidates asks them for a name, they may mention yours.

Appoint one of your network buddies as your career development mentor. Discuss any significant developments at work that might be a threat or an opportunity for you (e.g. a major reorganisation). Plot your next move between you.

Be sure to develop a good working relationship with your boss and key members of your company's management team. In four out of five promotions, the successful candidate has a mentoring relationship with a senior member of the management team who recommends them to colleagues.

Maintain a good reputation
Your reputation goes before you so maintain its currency by behaving professionally, whatever your boss, colleagues or life in general might throw at you. When things don't go your way, learn what lessons you can and move on positively. Put your name about by speaking at industry events and writing features for a trade paper or website.

Take the initiative and raise your profile
Don't always wait for someone to suggest your next move. If you spot a weak point in your company's competitive position or a way to show rivals a clean pair of heels, take a chance and seize the opportunity for yourself. Before you present your suggestion, do a quick business case study to check out the scale of opportunity and any investment required, in anticipation of your boss's objections.

Networking

> **Here's an idea for you...**
>
> Become the company scout. Sniffing out the competition is a great way to keep your eye on new opportunities. You may raise eyebrows within your own company but it's actually useful for them to know what their rivals are doing. Position yourself to take part in industry events like conferences and seminars where you'll meet your opposite numbers from companies in your sector. If your company operates in a scientific or technical field, check out the latest patent applications and see who filed them.

Modesty won't get you very far. If people don't know about you and your capabilities, how are they going to be on your side? Let them know about your progress and your ambitions. To some extent, it's a numbers game: the more people that know you and your reputation, the more often your name is likely to pop up when opportunities are discussed.

Keep people in touch with your progress and let them know about major achievements, like a promotion or completion of a big project. Get in touch with the websites and trade papers that cover your sector and send a press release when you have something that will interest their readers.

Hunt in a pack

Some of the best moves come from being part of a team that moves from one organisation to the next as a result of being recognised for its expertise in a particular area. For example, a specialist team moves from bank to bank upgrading their IT systems.

Idea 26 – **Make contacts before you're ready for a change**

Be ready to hit the ground running
You have to be ready to take advantage of the next opportunity. That means staying ahead of the competition by developing your skills and knowledge; it's not enough to stay ahead of the pack in your field, you have to anticipate your next promotion or move so that you're ready to make a contribution from day one.

Past achievements may not always predict future performance but it's always useful to have your CV ready to submit at short notice if necessary – you might be too busy to compile it otherwise. Keep it up to date. The regular updating exercise will help you recognise your own achievements and remind you whether your career is on track.

Timing is everything. Get the right skills required for your next job before you need them — then you'll be positioned when the time is right. Jane Ackerman, Raytheon Electronic Systems

How did it go?

Q. I see a reorganisation on the horizon. There are quiet conversations in the corridor and they've called in the consultants. Should I stay or should I go?

A. Well spotted: your 'reorganisation radar' has given you time to identify some options, which is always better than a nasty surprise. Weigh up the options in terms of what's best for you – loyalty, unfortunately, is rarely rewarded. Do what's best for your long-term future. Compare the value of any pay-off you would be entitled to if you are a candidate for redundancy against the increased difficulty of finding another job once people know you are available. It's generally easier to find a job when you already have one – especially as you get older.

Q. I've been looking for a move for some time but the best offer I've had so far is not an obvious promotion – it's more of a sideways move. Won't that look bad on my CV?

A. It's your career path and a sideways move may be just what you need. Move to a large company for experience managing bigger budgets. Try a SME (small/medium-size enterprise) for more rounded experience. One girl left her well-paid job as a consultant to join a client permanently because she decided it was the right time in her career to get hands-on, in-depth experience instead of a superficial knowledge of a great many projects.

27. Masters of their craft

Don't overlook the networks that have been around for years such as your local chamber of commerce or trade association.

The perfect way to start building networking relationships is in a low-key, undemanding and supportive environment.

That's just what you can find among long-standing networks in your community. You can get involved in anything from a global initiative to fund-raising for the local hospice. These groups offer a friendly welcome and members with lots of experience of life and work.

Associations with a future
Chambers of commerce serve the interests of local traders and support local business initiatives. But as a national organisation they also represent the views of their members to government and have a lobbying function (e.g. on taxation for small businesses). Some voluntary organisations manage to combine service to the local community with an international dimension, which provides great scope for networking. The Lions (www.lionsclubs.org) say: 'We meet the needs of our local communities and the world.' It is an international network of more than 1 million young men and women in 200 countries. Members take part in a vast variety of projects, ranging from cleaning up local parks to providing supplies to victims of natural disasters.

Networking

Here's an idea for you...

Turn yourself into an informal spokesperson for your company. Look for a trade association or local interest group that works in your employer's sector and work on becoming your company's representative. Then you could send out emails along the lines: 'At the meeting last night, they asked for recommendations on companies that might be willing to host visiting speakers from foreign companies. If you're interested, send me an email.' Suddenly you've made yourself an informal company spokesperson, which will be seen as you showing leadership qualities.

Rotary International (www.ribi.org) is a global network of business and professional people with 1.2 million members in 168 countries. Clubs in small towns may have just a dozen or so members, while those in large cities have hundreds. They meet on a regular basis, which allows members to build firm friendships. Some concentrate on local community projects while others link up with a sister club in another country to undertake an international project. Every member of Rotary has a right to attend any club meeting anywhere in the world, so there is always somewhere to go and people to meet, wherever you travel.

Online networking clubs like Ecademy (www.ecademy.com) and Linked-In (www.linkedin.com) – which aim at putting business people in touch via the internet – sometimes also run face-to-face networking events for members in particular cities.

Work your apprenticeship

What these associations have in common is that they can offer you a warm welcome and a collegiate ambiance where you have the opportunity to network at your own pace. You can hone your networking skills in a sympathetic forum, where people are generally more than willing to pass on the benefit of their years of experience to younger members. Such environments are also a place to find reliable suppliers of business services and meet potential customers – directly and from referrals.

Idea 27 – **Masters of their craft**

The main thing to remember is that this is a sympathetic environment. Don't wait for other members to come to you. Take the initiative and go over to a group who are already talking among themselves. Just join in and follow the conversation that's already going on. Wait to introduce yourself until there's a gap in the conversation – people's body language will tell you when it's time to step forward and say who you are and what you do. A smile and a warm manner will show that you're friendly. They want to share their experiences – particularly their successes – and views on life. Listen actively and ask questions that allow them a chance to talk from that experience, such as:

- What advice would you give someone just starting out on their career today?
- What's the greatest change you have seen in your business profession over the years?
- What's the biggest surprise you've experienced in your business profession?

People love sharing their experiences but often don't have the chance to do so. Encourage them to reminisce – and learn from their mistakes. Show respect for their experience and give them the chance to do some mentoring; you're never too old, or too young, to take advice.

Life can only be understood backward, but it must be lived forward.

Søren Kierkegaard, nineteenth-century Danish philosopher and theologian

Networking

How did it go?

Q. I would like to attend a networking meeting but I know my boss would say it's a waste of time and I should concentrate on doing my work. Any solution?

A. Follow the old adage: 'Ask for forgiveness rather than permission' – and be ready for the consequences. Sadly, some bosses have status issues around who attends outside events. Many regard themselves as the only suitable representative of the organisation and feel that their position is undermined if anyone else attends. Sometimes you have to take the initiative and be ready to justify your decision. Make sure there are some real benefits that you can point to for your organisation other than your own advancement.

Q. I've had a poor run at work recently and would like to get back on track in time for my next performance review. Would a mentor help?

A. Yes, it could help you break out of this cycle. Find one of your networking contacts that has 'been there, done that' in your industry sector and has good contacts. They might well see something of themselves in you and be willing to help you achieve your potential, or at least get you back on track. Some people refer to someone in this role as their 'elder lemon', a mark of respect that this is someone who has had the sour taste of bitter experience and learnt from it.

28. Start your own networking group

Take the chance to display those leadership and organisational skills – it's the perfect excuse to introduce yourself to all those individuals you've been dying to meet.

Remember that it doesn't have to be explicitly about career development. As long as you're passionate about it, you'll have the determination to make it succeed.

To create your network, set out to do something that matters to you. Local issues are a good place to start: people feel strongly about what affects them directly. For instance, there are networks dedicated to property prices, bartering, baby-sitting, plumbing services, local politics – almost everything, in fact. You benefit from the proximity, as neighbours can swap advice and support over a cup of coffee.

If you don't feel you can just go round and take the first step with your neighbours, try reaching out to people online. Many people are happier to take the first step online rather than face to face. Once they have, they usually grow more confident and enthusiastic about interacting with others. In fact, more than 50% of online networking traffic is purely social as people discover how much they enjoy getting to make new friends.

Here's an idea for you...

If the prospect of setting up an entire networking group seems too daunting, why not start small? Almost everyone would benefit from having a mentor, a trusted friend and adviser who acts as a kind of sounding board for problems or tricky decisions. It's a two-way street: at times you look for support while at others you provide it for your co-mentor. If you don't know anyone to be your mentor, there are plenty of existing business and social mentoring schemes you can join (e.g. the Mentoring and Befriending Foundation).

Team up

If you really want to get organised, you might need help – practical help plus the emotional support that will see you through the inevitable setbacks. Find two or three others who feel as strongly as you and who will share part of the responsibility and organising effort.

Your new network will take your total commitment so don't forget to keep your nearest and dearest on board. Warn them in advance or else they may feel sidelined as your networking consumes ever more of your time and energy. Actually, they may benefit in the longer term if your networking efforts lead to higher earnings or a livelier social life. So, talk through your plans realistically with them and check that they will support you or – at least – put up with your new interest.

Use networking to decide on your next career move

If you're not sure about your next career move, but know it's time for a change, why not make a start and use your network to help you decide your career direction?

Follow the example of Stephanie Cabot, who was a 'reluctant banker' at JP Morgan. She wanted a change but wasn't sure what she'd like to do next. She made a list of her 30 most promising career ideas and contacted everyone she could think of who was already working in one of her chosen fields. She asked each of them if she could meet up to pick their brains about their sector and what they liked and disliked about their work.

The response was very good because she wasn't asking for a job, just for tips for someone like herself who was thinking about moving into the area. One of these contacts was an author, who had no agent and wanted help editing and selling a book he was writing. Stephanie promised him she would help and with advice from a contact in publishing she used her social skills to contact publishers. She eventually generated interest from three of them, which sparked a bidding war and a six-figure contract for the author. The experience convinced her to seek her next career step in publishing. Impressed with her achievement, the William Morris Agency offered her a job as a literary agent and within five years she rose to become managing director.

> *I wanted to start a network of ethical, warm, kind people, people with a giving attitude, one where anyone that joined could feel warmth and a code of conduct that they would want to live up to. We call it 'winning by sharing'.*
>
> Penny Power, founder of Ecademy

How did it go?

Q. I'm new to the idea of networking and wondering where I should start. Any examples?

A. One enterprising female executive created a female-only lunch club. She invited all the senior women she had met through work and asked them to bring one friend along with them. At a stroke she doubled the number of her contacts.

Q. I'm trying to set up my own network group. What kind of people should I look for in my management team?

A. Someone with exceptional knowledge and access to contacts can make a critical difference to your chances of success. For example, if your network is concerned with local issues, try to get someone on board who knows a lot about the local community, such as an estate agent or property finder. Most successful teams also need a 'cornerstone', a chairman-like figure who can resolve disputes and carry the group along in a clear direction. It's up to you to show the leadership that will inspire others to join you and recruit new networking buddies to a common cause.

Q. I've made a promising start with my networking group. How do I go about building it faster?

A. Look for other networking groups with a natural fit to your own and see if the founder wants to talk about a joint initiative (e.g. running an event together). If it goes well, you might find it suits both of you to collaborate more extensively and share your administrative costs. The fit may involve a similar aim, such as career development or complementary industry sectors (e.g. PR and marketing).

Idea 28 – **Start your own networking group**

29. Power play

Corporate teambuilding and networking events can boost your profile when you grab the opportunities.

From line dancing to orienteering, teambuilding exercises can bring real benefits to your company and to you personally. Just make sure you set your own agenda carefully.

Before the day arrives, you should think carefully about what you want to get out of a corporate teambuilding event. If you don't have a clear goal in mind at the start, it will be hard to know what you have achieved. It should be more than an expenses-paid day out of the office.

Keep in step
The company agenda for activities of this kind is generally to improve team spirit and performance; to see who is capable of leadership and who has the sort of skills and aptitudes that make them suitable to be let loose in customer facing roles.

Your own agenda may be rather more modest: you may be into damage limitation, afraid that whatever activity is involved will stretch your talent beyond its limits. Or you may be concerned about how you will cope with the loss of time that a day – or more – out of the office represents. Nevertheless, you may as well make an effort to embrace what you can't escape.

See the day as an opportunity. It is a way to meet colleagues from other parts of the organisation, to make contact with people who might prove to be a useful ally and could become part of your own network – possibly even an informal mentor. It's also good training for your 'soft' skills, like communication and people management, and ideal for developing customer service skills or pitching for business.

Stretching times

The day could test your endurance in quite unexpected ways. It's not just the physical and mental testing that the official teambuilding exercise will put you through. You will have to cope outside your comfort zone, cut adrift from your normal pattern back at the ranch and those well-established little routines that make life there bearable. You will be on show more visibly and continuously than is usual. You will have to demonstrate some attempt to support your colleagues and do your bit for the team.

You could be travelling, eating and – heaven forbid – sleeping with your colleagues as well as working together on team exercises. Spending all this time together might produce some surprises. That 'techie' from support might display some previously well-hidden leadership qualities while a colleague you had barely noticed before might turn out to look surprisingly fit in sweaty shorts.

> *Here's an idea for you...*
>
> Volunteer! Take on responsibility for running an event. By taking ownership you will get more out of it. Ask your colleagues for ideas about the type of activity they want to do and involve them in organising the event, like booking the venue. Minimise the risk of getting the blame if the day proves unpopular by setting realistic expectations and – if the budget allows – hiring an external trainer.

Networking

But it's also likely that on top of the demands of the actual exercises, the enforced contact and possibly limited facilities will lead to something close to 'cabin fever', a kind of group claustrophobia. Your colleagues will start to irritate you (and – shock, horror – vice versa).

Pass the audition
Grit your teeth! Smile. Stay as well-groomed as you can in these trying circumstances. Think of this as a down-payment on your next promotion. Whatever the provocation, resist the temptation to rebel or, worse still, sulk. Avoid even the slightest signs of alcoholic hangover or romance; those 'we're just comparing hotel rooms' excuses won't wash.

Chorus line
Stand out when the competition is at its strongest. Do what it takes to get to know the right people – you need to get known throughout the company. If you're asked to head up a committee, for example, select people *outside* your group, especially people you think it might be useful to work with in future.

Once you are on the company 'grapevine' you'll get to know about the latest developments and openings sooner than most, giving you a head start on the route to future promotions and pay rises.

Coming together is a beginning. Keeping together is progress. Working together is success. Henry Ford

How did it go?

Q. A new recruit is joining my team. How do I integrate them as quickly and smoothly as possible?

A. Be careful not succumb to the temptation to compare your new team member with the person they replaced. You may regret the loss of a known quantity and team-mate but new people often have a fresh outlook that helps revive enthusiasm. To get new team members off to a good start, make sure they fully understand what their role entails. If possible try to arrange for their first few days on the job to overlap with the notice period of a departing colleague, who can show them the ropes and also introduce them to colleagues in other departments, clients and suppliers, which helps speed up the relationship-building process.

Q. One of my colleagues is a real ditherer. How can I get a decision out of her?

A. People with a tendency to put off decision-making are usually poor communicators. They fail to realise that at some point a decision – almost any decision – is better than none. They often hold back because they are uncertain of their own ability and other people's confidence in them. You see hesitation in what they say and how they say it. When you spot the body language, encourage her to open up about her reservations. Once you've identified the problem, help her examine the facts and review the main options. Then give her plenty of support when she does reach a decision.

30. The power of words

There's nothing like public speaking or writing to show you are one of your sector's leading thinkers. It's not as tricky as it sounds, either, if you stick to these proven techniques.

Carve out a reputation as a thought-leader in your industry by speaking at events and writing for trade publications. Aim to spend around 5% of your time doing your own PR.

Find your voice
Have your say at work. How often have you sat there in a meeting waiting for a chance to tell everyone your suggestion, when someone else makes almost exactly the same point and wins everyone's approval?

Take a chance and speak out – say what you honestly think. People may not instantly agree with your ideas but at least you are giving voice to them. As long as you remain silent, those ideas remain untested. Anyway, you will feel better about yourself if you have had your say, which will help build your confidence.

Your self-belief will give conviction to what you say and write. The same quality will go a long way towards carrying your audience along with you when you make a presentation or write an article. Your case has to stand up, of course.

Pitching

Be clear about the problem you are addressing and convinced about your solution. What are you trying to achieve? Is your aim to convince your audience about a new trend in your industry or a new course of action for the business? Check the validity of the case by arguing it through with colleagues.

Think about your audience. For a verbal presentation, you are competing for their attention – 20 minutes is the limit for most people. Anticipate their likely objections and deal with them. If you are looking for a collective decision, it's best to lobby key decision makers individually in advance; ask them what you have to do to gain their support.

Bear in mind yours is not the only project on their agenda. What other projects are competing for resources? Who else might they want to run the project? Remember to get the benefits in front of your audience as soon as you begin and don't be afraid to repeat them. For example, if you are asking your boss for an assistant, emphasise the enhanced status and work rate the new appointment will bring to the team. Asking the board to authorise a £1 million project? Focus on the payback, the 300% return on investment the project will deliver. For each message that you want to convey, use an example that will relate to your audience. Deliver the 'foghorn message' clearly. It should run throughout a verbal presentation and any paperwork; announce it with a phrase like 'if there's one thing you take away from this, it's …'

> *Here's an idea for you…*
>
> Practise having your say in situations where you feel most confident. For example, go to your favourite store and try on racks of clothes, without buying a single thing. Without being rude, find genuine reasons to turn down each and every item, however painful this is for you. Resolve to translate this attitude into your working life – the next time you disagree with something, put your own view across just as politely but firmly as you did in the store.

Use the company's proper submission process and double check how long you have to present your case. You may still be interrupted or cut short, so be prepared. Spell out exactly what you are seeking agreement on and the next steps. Welcome feedback: make it clear if you want to take questions during your talk or at the end; repeat each question asked before you reply, to make sure everybody heard it (and give yourself a little thinking time).

There are no absolute certainties, but if you take the time to make the case successfully, the chances are your company and your career will benefit.

The dos and don'ts for speaking in public
- Don't try to pack too much in – put the fine details in a hand-out.
- Smile, occasionally – too much can look like a desperate bid for acceptance.
- Keep breathing – stay connected with what's going on around you, as this will help you relax.
- Occupy your space – give yourself a moment to look around before you start to talk; spot someone you know in the audience or pause to take off your jacket to help you feel at home.
- Talk in a warm, open manner so people can understand you easily.
- Maintain eye contact throughout your presentation.

Language exerts hidden power, like a moon on the tides.

Rita Mae Brown, American screen writer, author and social activist

Idea 30 – **The power of words**

How did it go?

Q. I sometimes lose the thread when I speak in public and feel safer if I can go through a well-structured sequence of visuals. Is that OK?

A. Avoid using visuals as a safety net. They should reinforce your points, not act simply as an aid to your memory. Restrict them to graphs, diagrams and well-chosen pictures that illustrate your point. Three or four visuals are generally plenty for a 20-minute presentation slot. Put the main effort into structuring the argument so you can break off to deal with questions and come back to your flow. Glancing at notes used as a cue is okay but reading from the page or overhead visuals is a recipe for terminal boredom.

Q. How do I go about persuading trade publications to accept an article for publication?

A. Think about *their* audience. Most publications are hungry for a good story that will interest their readers. Pick titles whose readership most corresponds to your topic – the proliferation of magazines in print and on the web means you can target precisely. Contact a member of the editorial team and ask them if they will look at your story, then follow up to see how relevant they think it is to their readers. Keep plugging away until you produce something they accept.

137

31. Cast your net far and wide

Just because you're off duty doesn't mean you should be switched off – art fairs and sports venues are fabulous places to meet people.

Network while you work out at the gym, visit a fashion show or an exhibition of new artists' work.

In the office, most people are conscious of their status and want to maintain the working relationships that they have established as colleagues, clients or competitors. Outside the office, it may be a little different. It can be a lot easier to chat to your boss if both of you are pounding out the miles on adjacent running machines at the gym. All that stress-busting activity brings out another side of people.

It's the same with creative activities. Stephen Somerville, a long-serving presenter on the BBC's *Antiques Roadshow*, says that art serves to help people open up a bit more. 'A lot of people find it hard to come out of themselves,' he observes. 'You only have to go to a board meeting – it's all a bit of a performance. Art helps to make it okay to express emotion.'

Choose what turns your head
The range of corporate events is huge. As women's share of corporate spending has increased, organisers have had to think about what will attract them out of

the office during the day or away from their families in the evening. There are author appearances, shopping and make-up events as well as exclusive private viewings with fashion designers. Invitations to catwalk shows at fashion events are sought after. The great thing is that they do not take up a whole day of your time; they're brief, over in under an hour. But the level of anticipation and excitement is huge, which means that people attending them are at their most enthusiastic and open to new encounters. All of which makes them fantastic from a networking perspective.

> **Here's an idea for you...**
>
> Get chatting to your fellow passengers. Planes, boats and trains are a great place to make new contacts – everybody is looking for a way to pass the time, especially on a long journey. It's not just a chance to hone your networking skills, you never know who you may be sitting beside. It might just be a route into a new job or a new romance. Try a smile first; a response is a sign that a little gentle conversation is in order.

Be picky
If you work in the media or investment banking, you receive so many invitations for corporate 'dos' that you could spend every off-duty hour at one event or another. They may be fun and a good way to make new contacts but some are more valuable than others. People working in these sectors soon learn to pick and choose which are likely to be worth their while to attend.

Take a tip from them and be picky. The real test of a successful event is one where you have the chance to meet and interact with high-profile, interesting and influential people. See if you can check out the guest list in advance by having a word with the organiser.

Network while you work out
Certainly, more and more people see exercise as stress-relieving and motivating. It creates a good atmosphere – somehow people in their trainers and sweatpants are much more themselves.

However, not every kind of activity is a great leveller. Sports can be quite 'macho'. The golf course has traditionally been the place for combining business with playing sport. The game even has a handicap system so that people of different levels of ability can still enjoy each other's company.

Fortunately, today's time-poor, health-conscious professional types are more likely to spend a power hour at the gym than devote an afternoon to golf. Stick to aerobics, dance classes or the gym where, unlike golf, there's no need for a handicap system.

These places are aimed squarely at the upwardly mobile. Generally, they are not cheap to join, which often means the membership is self-selecting. There is usually a high quota of professional types and you are bound to bump into colleagues and contacts; you may well meet your financial adviser and business mentor there, as well as your personal trainer. It's surprising how much business you can do over a glass of something refreshing in the bar.

> *To approach the stranger is to invite the unexpected, release a new force, let the genie out of the bottle. It is to start a new train of events that is beyond your control.* T. S. Eliot

Idea 31 – *Cast your net far and wide*

How did it go?

Q. I have to go to a lot of male-oriented company dos, like cricket matches, and all I seem to do is spend my time avoiding over-attentive and juvenile guys. How should we women deal with them?

A. Men do tend to create their own very special 'locker room' atmosphere, and expect everybody else to conform in terms of, for instance, drinking rituals and jokes, etc. Try to avoid criticising them in public; they'll even interpret a sensible suggestion as a rebuke. Any display of emotion will be taken as a sign of weakness so keep your cool. The tone of corporate events is usually set from the top, so look for support there, if necessary.

Q. The chance to network with colleagues or senior managers would be a fine thing. At my company everyone works or heads straight home. What can I do?

A. Take the initiative. Get together with a couple of colleagues and check out the local gyms and health spas, etc. Operators are generally happy to do a group deal on membership fees. Have a chat with the manager: is there a waiting list; are there special deals? If you're asking your company to subsidise membership fees, take a proposal to your boss and look for support to present it to the board or whoever would have to sign it off. Emphasise how much a quick lunchtime workout adds to productivity.

32. The 24/7 fallacy

Here is why putting in long, punishing hours on someone else's behalf does you no favours whatsoever.

It's hard to avoid the long-hours culture, but you can increase your capacity to cope with the stress. A sense of being in control works wonders for your motivation and peace of mind.

Embrace your corporate culture
The first forty hours you work in a week are usually the most productive, while the next ten, twenty or thirty will deliver a diminishing return. It's almost certainly the case for your colleagues, too, unless they come from another galaxy.

But that won't stop ambitious people putting in the hours at work. In many sectors, a company culture builds up that demands conspicuous effort in return for promotion and pay-rises. So, if your company has that culture, accept it; you're stuck with it for as long as you remain there. In fact, if you want to get on, embrace it wholeheartedly: work with it not against it. Just remember to warn your family and friends that your career means more to you than anything else. That way, you'll set realistic expectations about how much time you are going to spend with them – and they can make up their own minds about their own priorities.

Idea 32 – **The 24/7 fallacy**

Develop a capacity for stress

Longer working hours, short-term targets and the 'blame culture' all combine to increase stress levels at work, as well as specific working conditions such as too much – or too little – work or lack of support from managers.

There's no escape from it. Stress is part of our lives and keeps us alert and lively. But people need a level of pressure that's right for them. Behavioural experts say that we cope best with work pressures when we feel in control of our lives. It helps if you're valued, secure and well managed, too.

The key to dealing with stress is to see that you make the time to recover from it. That way, you develop a healthy capacity to cope with particularly busy periods. You can't work at peak demand without a break.

Be in control

Top-ranking professionals and managers have the least stress-related illness. It's people at the bottom of the pecking order that tend to have the highest levels because they have the least control over their working lives. A sense of control comes from having a degree of autonomy over your work and some flexibility in your schedule. Of course, this is more common in some sectors than others.

Flexible jobs

Many women have to cope with having a family while still holding their own with their peers at work. And that tends to happen in their late twenties and early

> *Here's an idea for you...*
>
> Think about what you can delegate. We're not just talking about giving some more of your paperwork to an assistant – they are probably overworked, too. Can your mother collect the kids from school now and again? Can you order your groceries online instead of visiting the shops? How about outsourcing some of the household chores, like ironing, to a friend, student or neighbour? These services will cost you something but is doing these petty chores more important than fulfilling your ambitions?

143

Networking

thirties when pressure to fit in with peers is probably at its greatest. It helps if you work in a sector where competition for talent leads to flexible working conditions.

Jane Butler rose to become Cisco's top woman in Europe. As director of the computer company's consulting business, Butler led a team of 91 technical consultants and system engineers. Her own early experience of managing conflicting pressures – 'I even learnt to breast-feed and type at the same time' – has given Butler an insight into how to manage her own career and mentor others.

'If you have the freedom that you don't always have to go into the office at eight in the morning and leave at five,' she says, 'then you can fit a family life around a working life – because babies tend to be 24-hour beasts. You may not get much sleep or social life, but you can juggle them.'

In her own case, Butler feels that the fact that her job does not always require a routine day in the office has helped her fit so much in. She believes this is a big advantage of the IT industry for women.

> Time is the coin of your life. It is the only coin you have, and only you can determine how it will be spent. Be careful lest you let other people spend it for you. Carl Sandburg, American author

Idea 32 – **The 24/7 fallacy**

How did it go?

Q. I have very little time to spare but I would like to test out the benefits of networking. I'm tempted to try one of these online networking or mentoring sites. What do you think of them?

A. They are a bit hit and miss, quite frankly. The problem is that successful networking and mentoring depends on establishing relationships of trust with people. This takes time, I'm afraid; there's just no getting away from it. You could be lucky, but visiting a network group in person is probably faster in the long run because you can tell if there's a rapport much more quickly in the flesh.

Q. I'm struggling to juggle the demands of home and career, so I'm wondering if I might as well go the whole way and start up my own business. Are the rewards worth all the effort?

A. Will it make you happy? That's the real issue, because you would almost certainly find yourself juggling even more. The big advantage – if you make a success of it – is that you feel in control of your own destiny, which is highly motivating and rewarding. It would certainly be hard work but you might decide that running your own business is the only choice that offers you the chance to claw back a balance between work, time for your family and time for yourself.

Networking

33. Eat your way to the top

Don't skip meals: lunch is for winners not wimps.

Long, leisurely business lunches may have gone out with the bubble perm and big shoulder pads but that doesn't mean consuming food no longer plays a role in networking.

The current working environment may be more frenetic than 20 years ago but companies haven't stopped doing deals over meals. If you are entertaining a client outside the office, make a reservation at a restaurant that is convenient for you both to get to. Nowadays plenty of restaurants guarantee to serve you two courses within an hour and choosing one of those shows respect for your client's time. It's also worth bearing in mind that for many, two courses is now a long meal. If you are dining with clients in the evening, preferably book early, ideally around 7 p.m., because they may have families to go home to or an early start next day.

Networking

Here's an idea for you…

It may be a bit non-Anglo-Saxon but chit-chat about food and drink is a great ice breaker. So, the next time you find the pleasantries flagging at an event, try talking about something tasty to get the conversation flowing again. Have you checked out the new wine club being advertised at the moment? What do you think of the Japanese restaurant that's opened up around the corner?

Pick a restaurant you're familiar with where they'll treat you with respect as a host. Find out if your client is vegetarian or has any allergies or religious dietary requirements that you'll need to consider when you're making your choice. The food should be good but not unusually exotic: this isn't a gastronomic adventure. It's also worth remembering that spending a fortune on a meal might create the impression your company wastes money.

You want to hear each other but not be overheard, as you may have a confidential discussion over the meal. Consequently the noise level should be low and there should be plenty of space between the tables. Over-attentive staff who interrupt your conversation every five minutes to ask if everything is all right or refill glasses are another potential irritant to be wary of.

Since you did the inviting, you set the pace of the meal. Nowadays, most people prefer mineral water to wine at lunchtime but you can order a bottle of wine to go with dinner. Always say if you're having a starter or dessert as well as a main so your guest can take their cue from you. Let everyone relax and order their food before you get down to business. Ask for the bill at the same time as dessert and coffee – if you're having any – to save time. As the host, you pay – preferably by credit card to keep a record for the tax man and to avoid any awkward questions over the bill.

Idea 33 – **Eat your way to the top**

Since everyone is so time-poor these days, a new lead or contact may resist meeting you for lunch or dinner. However, face-to-face time is important if you're to build up trust and establish a relationship, so you might try suggesting that you meet for a coffee or a quick drink after work instead. Breakfast meetings are popular with some people because the fixed time slot implies a brisk discussion.

When you are invited out for a business meal, follow your host's lead in terms of courses, drink and cost. This is not an occasion to linger over a meal but don't rush things either. Always send a note or email thanking them for their hospitality afterwards. Very lavish affairs may merit a thank-you gift, such as flowers, as well.

Don't forget that meal times at your workplace are a major networking opportunity, too. Even if it's hard at times to tear yourself away from your desk, if you have an office canteen or your colleagues pop out for a sandwich, make sure you join them on a regular basis. Not only will you strengthen relationships but you will also keep abreast of gossip and learn about openings. These get-togethers are often an unofficial recruiting ground and a great opportunity to get senior colleagues and people from other departments on side.

A dinner lubricates business.

Lord William Stowell, prominent eighteenth-century English judge

Networking

How did it go?

Q. Help! A friend has offered to introduce me to her boss, who I'm dying to talk to. They want to meet at an oyster bar and I have never eaten oysters before. Any tips?

A. Be a good sport and give oysters a try. They'll show you how. If you then find they're not to your liking don't dwell on the fact and quietly order an alternative dish. Your friend and her boss are clearly enthusiasts, otherwise they wouldn't have invited you to join them at an oyster bar in the first place.

Q. If I take contacts out to a fancy restaurant to thank them for a favour and the meal is terrible, what should I do?

A. Your contacts will feel as embarrassed as you do. Don't make it worse by 'having it out' with the staff in front of them. Speak to the manager afterwards in private about why the food was sub-standard. Then invite your contacts out for another meal at a restaurant of their choosing.

Q. I am on a diet and my company is holding a gala dinner for clients. Is there any way to get out of eating?

A. At this dinner you are a host – an ambassador for your company. By skipping the food you will become the focus of negative attention and could spoil your guests' enjoyment of their meal. You'll have to eat the first two courses but you are allowed to pass on dessert and cheese as you are 'full'.

34. Charitable giving

By doing charity work, not only will you help others, you could also potentially make useful contacts and learn new career-enhancing skills.

Volunteering can bring big rewards as well as a strong sense of accomplishment from doing a good deed. It can really help your personal development plan, too.

Volunteering is great way to meet people

The first thing you hear volunteers talking about – apart from how much they enjoy helping others – is how they meet so many genuine caring individuals. When you decide to give your time to a charitable organisation, you already have something in common with the other volunteers – you all support the cause. This makes it much easier to connect with the team, who will most probably come from a variety of backgrounds. But volunteering doesn't just help you make new friends. It brings new contacts that can change your career. Raising awareness of a cause you believe in can put you in touch with senior professionals and captains of industry. Your community spirit will hold you in good stead: it tells an employer that you are a team player with social skills and a great attitude.

Gain transferable skills by volunteering

Volunteering for a charitable organisation is a fabulous way to gain work experience, for students, those in their first jobs – in fact for people at every stage

Networking

Here's an idea for you...

If you have found no time so far, the speediest way to combine good-deed-doing and networking is to host a fund-raising party for your favourite cause. Create a buzz around your event with a theme like 'Jazz-age cocktails at six', or have a VIP speaker who is sure to bring in the crowds. Charge your friends admission and ask them to bring someone new. You'll have some fun and meet lots of different people.

in their career. The so-called 'soft skills', like good communication and negotiation, are increasingly valued in today's workplace. Volunteering is a great way to improve them. If you are on your way up the corporate ladder, a voluntary project can help you acquire the management ability needed for future promotions and pay rises.

Maybe you're looking for a complete change or a way to boost your confidence when you're making the transition back into work after a break. Volunteering lets you try something out and decide if you really want to work in that sector. Last, but not least, it also looks good on your CV.

In the rapidly globalising economy, companies, especially multinationals, seek people with international knowledge. Charitable work abroad is an excellent way to gain that experience. You will see other countries in a way that you would never have been able to as a tourist. You learn to mix well and develop self-reliance.

Volunteering overseas proves you are open-minded and capable of adapting to another culture, another way of doing things. It shows employers you've developed some understanding of how other nations approach business.

Volunteering shows you're a multitasker
The pace of business is faster than ever these days and everyone puts in longer hours. If you can cope with the pressures of a demanding job and still make time

for a worthwhile cause it shows you want to make a positive difference to the wider community.

Building up your organisational abilities through volunteering makes you a more attractive employee. Nowadays employers aren't just looking for hard workers. They want people with the capacity to go that extra mile and juggle several balls at once. Doing voluntary work on top of everything else shows that you are a confident multitasker committed to getting projects done. It demonstrates you are highly motivated and willing to try something new.

Businesses get very excited about people who have a passionate belief and the initiative to work for a worthwhile cause – if necessary without payment. Some, especially larger businesses, have started to set up time-banking schemes, where you commit a fixed number of hours a week to a voluntary or charitable activity. Your voluntary activities can even become part of your annual appraisal if your company wants to encourage a culture of volunteering among its workforce.

The result is a win–win situation where employees feel good about the company they work for and also have the time for voluntary work that means a lot to them. But it isn't just a case of businesses favouring employees who do their bit for charity. Increasingly, people prefer to choose to make a career within an organisation that takes social responsibility seriously – including a commitment to volunteering.

No act of kindness, no matter how small, is ever wasted. Aesop, Ancient Greek storyteller

How did it go?

Q. I've been volunteering with older people who don't always hear so well. Any tips on how to communicate better with them?

A. As you're already aware you'll need to be a bit more patient and considerate when you talk to people who have trouble hearing because they can easily lose the thread of conversation. Face them and maintain eye contact. Let them see your mouth forming words even if they can't lip-read. Slow down your rate of speech and turn up the volume without shouting. Find out if they have a 'good ear' and sit on that side. Fill them in on conversations that are taking place around you and distractions like public announcements. Don't give up when the going gets tough. Resort to pen and paper if necessary.

Q. I work for a small business and don't have much free time but I'd still like to get involved in a good cause. Any suggestions?

A. With today's busy schedule, it's increasingly difficult for many people to make a regular commitment to voluntary work. That's why charities such as Community Service Volunteers now offer one-off weekend projects, like maintaining the grounds of a care home. You might also think about doing some voluntary work abroad during your holidays. There are a number of travel organisations that match your skills to project needs and will arrange a volunteering holiday for you. These trips can be as short as five days.

35. Schmoozing for students

Paper qualifications aren't the whole story. Here's how to end up with something to show for your education.

It takes more than a degree to land a plum job once you graduate. Socialise proactively while you're studying and you'll be in pole position to get to where you want to go.

With so many graduates to choose from these days, recruiters aren't merely interested in good marks. Graduates who gain experience in the real world have far more to offer businesses than those who simply absorbed academic theory. People skills and communication skills come top of employers' shopping lists. Whether you want to be a lawyer or you're still trying to decide between banking and management consultancy, it's vital you learn to interact well with others.

Good relationships are totally transferable – one of the few things you can take with you wherever you go from job to job. Knowing you have a strong network in place when you need support is invaluable to your career as well as all other aspects of your life. University is an ideal environment in which to begin nurturing these bonds. So, make the most of extra-curricular activities. The sooner you are involved, the faster you'll gain a footing on your career path.

Capitalise on the university career services and job fairs

Some university career services are better equipped to help you than others. It depends where you are studying and what you intend to pursue as a career. Nevertheless, it's a place to start. They all offer workshops on preparing your CV and applying for jobs; the mock interview sessions can only enhance your prospects. Individual guidance sessions are as useful as you make them. It's up to you to drive the discussion, so come prepared. For example, ask the adviser for pointers on how to find a work placement in your chosen field.

Career service departments organise recruitment fairs, events and presentations. It's wise to attend a selection of these events, even if you don't think you fit the mould for the candidates that businesses want to interview. It's a highly efficient way to find out what employers are looking for and willing to offer. You can use them to definitively eliminate certain companies or industry sectors from your enquiries; and it's also a fabulous opportunity to practise those networking skills on company recruiters.

Work experience

Work experience is a must while you're in university because it maximises the opportunity of a longer-term association. Do some preparation. Look on the web and on the newspapers' careers pages for information on professions and companies that interest you. For an in-depth insight, arrange a meeting with an employee or graduate recruitment officer – your career service can advise you how to approach them. Develop contacts and skills by becoming a 'work-shadow', participating in a work placement, or winning a place on an internship scheme.

Another way to develop the people skills that businesses really want is by volunteering for charities. Employers like to see a spell with a voluntary organisation on your CV not just because it shows a sense of community responsibility but also because working with these organisations can help develop empathy and communication skills.

Join university clubs and societies

Student organisations and sports teams can teach you skills you can't pick up in the classroom, such as teamwork and the ability to negotiate and influence. However, don't simply set out to join every group going. It is important to work with others to achieve something (e.g. produce a video for a student film festival or fund-raise for a language trip to Italy).

If your university has an alumni network and mentoring scheme, be sure to take advantage of them. They help make the transition from classroom to work easier by offering ready-made contacts and one-to-one counselling, just what you need when you are starting out.

> **Here's an idea for you...**
>
> A run-of-the-mill job can look good on your CV. You can learn a lot from that part-time job in retail or behind a bar. Okay, it's not as glamorous as an internship with a leading computer firm, but you can spell out how it gave you early responsibility. Did it help hone your customer service skills? Did you deal with return of goods when the manager was off sick? Did you organise and promote musical events at the pub where you worked? It's how you make what you do count that interests graduate recruiters.

A college degree is not a sign that one is a finished product but an indication a person is prepared for life.

Reverend Edward A. Malloy, American writer and president of Notre Dame University

Networking

How did it go?

Q. I have no idea what I want to do for a living so how can I possibly go and gain any experience?

A. The worst thing you can do is nothing. Don't just stick your head in the sand and hope inspiration will come to you. Get involved in something, whether it's a work placement or volunteering for a charity. Talk to professionals in fields that interest you. Visit job fairs to gather information on possible careers. The more contacts you make, the more networking you do, the more you'll find out what's for you and what's not. Plus you'll know people who can help you when you're closer to making that decision.

Q. My parents have promised to pay for a trip abroad if I get good grades. How will this affect my job prospects?

A. If you plan to spend your entire vacation flat on your back on a beach, you won't be doing yourself any favours. However, if you spend the break as a camp counsellor in America or as a roadie on a band's European tour, you'll enhance your career prospects. Working holidays such as these show potential employers you've got organisational and people management skills as well as the ability to work in a team. Likewise, volunteering overseas adds lustre to your CV. Not only is it an opportunity to meet and work with diverse people, it demonstrates a sense of social responsibility.

36. Make the 'freebies' pay

Get the most out of work placements and internships.

Your task may range from a challenging research project to making the coffee; pay non-existent. Nevertheless, you get out what you put in to your work experience.

You've done the research, been to the job fairs and started to build up a picture of what you'd like to do. Now it's up to you to acquire the experience and skills that ensure you get a foot in the door of your chosen career. But be warned: the prospect of an exciting job at the end of the rainbow means there's lots of competition – even for unpaid work placements.

Preparation
You'll have to put in a great deal of preparation. Start early. Give yourself plenty of time to find the help you need and avoid becoming bogged down by assignments and exams. Research your target organisations as if you were applying for a job with them. Check the website for profiles of recent recruits and news of their progress. Perhaps you can contact them and arrange to meet them in person – it's the best way to form a realistic impression of the business and its culture.

> ### Here's an idea for you...
>
> Start as you mean to go on. Before you enter the premises on your first day of a work placement, take a moment to compose yourself. Stretch your spine, drop your shoulders and relax your facial muscles to relieve tension. Now stride in as confidently as you can. Greet everyone with a warm, friendly smile and a firm handshake. You may still feel incredibly nervous but you're off to a great start.

Large organisations have rigorous application processes for their work experience schemes, both paid and unpaid. They often put you through multiple interviews and aptitude tests if you're trying to land an internship or a placement that's part of your degree programme. Your university career service should be able to advise you how to prepare.

Plan a well thought-out campaign. You'll need to be persistent, particularly if you're trying to organise a work placement with a smaller employer that does not have an established application procedure. Contact them by phone, in writing and in person, so they realise you are serious. You may not win a place with your first choice but you are developing skills that will eventually pay off.

On the work placement

Before you start a work placement or an internship, it's a wise idea to arrange a visit to meet the team and familiarise yourself with your new surroundings. It will give you a flavour of the office atmosphere and dress code. Make sure you know when, where and to whom you have to report on your first day. If you have any questions, call the organiser or student liaison officer and ask them to answer your queries. Arrive in plenty of time on the day.

While on work experience you want to absorb as much as you can, so keep those eyes and ears open. You wouldn't want to disturb others unnecessarily when they're busy and you need to show you can work independently. But don't just sit there like a wallflower, content with the tasks you're given. Take every opportunity to get involved. Ask lots of questions when people have the time for a discussion; the lunch break is a good time to chat about working in the industry with members of the team. See if they'll let you attend team meetings or take part in brainstorms. You might just offer a fresh perspective. The more you make it clear this sector excites you, the more an employer will take notice of your ambition.

This is a chance to start developing professional relationships, so be friendly with everyone. Supervisors may let you know about future openings. Co-workers will move on to new jobs where they could introduce you to new opportunities. Even those pesky rivals – other work placement students – can help increase your knowledge and contacts. It should be easy to connect since you already have something in common.

Before you leave, make sure you ask for feedback on your performance. It's an opportunity to learn about the career skills you'll need to develop in order to make an impact. Then find a reason to arrange a return visit, such as to hear the results of a project that you have worked on. As a familiar face, you're more likely to end up with a job.

> Success in business requires training and discipline and hard work. But if you're not frightened by these things, the opportunities are just as great today as they ever were.

J. D. Rockefeller, American financier and statesman

How did it go?

Q. I'm feeling under-stretched on my work placement. The tasks are just so boring. How can I show them what I'm really capable of?

A. Take the initiative. Apply that talent constructively and show some enthusiasm. The last thing you want to do is leave the business with an impression you consider the work beneath you. Even if you're assigned some mundane duties, you should still put every effort into your work. Propose a more interesting project that you know you could do, provided you have support. Look for a mentor who can help you achieve your goals. If you give 100%, others are more likely to recognise it when you're looking for a reference or a job.

Q. I'm a recent graduate with a business degree on a supermarket management trainee programme. Some of their long-serving staff seem to resent working with me. What's their problem?

A. In businesses where people traditionally work their way up from the shop floor, degree qualifications don't always count for much. To some staff, especially the older members, you're just a fast-tracked upstart with no experience. The higher starting salary graduate trainees usually receive for doing similar work may rankle with them. All that fancy theory you learnt at college could be rubbing them up the wrong way. Keep your head down. Prove you're a brilliant team player as well as a hard worker and you'll probably find they accept you better.

Idea 36 – **Make the 'freebies' pay**

37. Leave a clean web footprint

If the information about you on the web isn't squeaky clean, it could lose you a job – or a cherished relationship.

> Be extremely sensible about what you post on the web — it's the very information that you most dread becoming public that often finds its way into the public domain, through the 'friend' of a 'friend'.

The web helps job seekers search out the jobs they want, circulate their CVs and generally raise their own profile. However, the power of the web cuts both ways. Many companies now outsource their recruitment almost entirely and much of the selection process starts online.

You may think that what you do in your spare time is none of their business and what's important is to have a solid CV and the best credentials for your next job. Anyway, you can always explain away any inconsistencies at the interview, can't you? No longer, unfortunately. You simply may not get the chance to explain in person those throw-away comments on your blog about the best way to skive off at work, or those snaps from the office party on your Facebook profile.

Avoid falling at the first fence

Don't forget that, at the first screening, a recruiter's task is to look for reasons to weed out candidates. Companies are finding that pre-employment checks are increasingly uninformative because employers are growing so cautious about what they say on references, restricting comments to factual data such as dates of employment. So a web search and a trawl of the social networking sites is becoming a routine part of that screening process.

Banks and other financial services organisations also routinely carry out a credit check on prospective employees, looking for signs of personal indebtedness, on the basis that you can hardly advise customers about managing their money if you can't manage your own.

> **Here's an idea for you...**
> Work at differentiating yourself from other candidates by ensuring favourable information comes up in the kind of quick internet trawl that recruiters carry out (e.g. look for a role in a charitable or voluntary organisation with a public face on the internet). It may be a struggle to fit in extra work with your other commitments but it could just give you the edge for that next job.

Manage your profile carefully

So, be sensible about what information you post on your own website and any social networking sites you join. Be as choosey about the people you befriend online as you would in the real world, otherwise you might find you've buddied up with someone whose profile is not genuine.

Some acquaintancies may be upset if you reject them but in the long run that might be the lesser of two evils: do you really want your boss to hear about everything you and your colleagues get up to outside work?

Make full use of the access settings that social networks provide; there's usually a privacy tab on the toolbar that lets you limit personal data to registered 'friends'.

Be careful about the tone of messages you post on someone else's page. A good rule of thumb is: if it's something you wouldn't say to their face, don't say it on their Facebook entry.

Play the recruiters at their own game
It's in your interest to:

- Make sure that your CV contains the key words that a potential employer is searching for when they carry out a search (e.g. industry specific skills).
- Post detailed and specific information about your skills and experience (e.g. name the training courses that you have been on, the number of days spent training and what difference it makes to your employability).
- Present yourself in the most favourable light. Screening is designed to eliminate candidates without the required qualifications – modesty won't improve your chances.

Never tell lies or exaggerate your experience or qualifications on your CV. Even if you get the job and remain employed, you'll always be scared that someone might reveal the truth.

Companies routinely check the web for background information on potential recruits so make sure your online presence is exemplary.

Sharon Lench, *PC Magazine*

Idea 37 – **Leave a clean web footprint**

How did it go?

Q. Loads of my friends already have signed up on MySpace and Facebook and they're on at me to sign up, too. What do I do?

A. Most people join social networking sites for the same reason as their friends – because everyone else is doing it. Then, once other people start messaging you, you feel you ought to reply and, hey presto, you start getting sucked in. So, you have to step back and decide if joining a particular site will enhance your presence on the web. You can enjoy most of the benefits of a higher web profile by joining one site only, which makes it easier to manage your online entries carefully. If you decide that signing up on another site is not in your interest, tell your friends that you're too busy to keep another entry up to date.

Q. How do I break the news to someone that I don't want to accept them as an online 'friend'?

A. Yes, you risk hurting someone's feelings when you say 'no'. But it's probably less of a blow than you might imagine – people typically ask practically everyone they know to sign up during their initial burst of enthusiasm for a new site, often using the automatic facility on the site to send emails to their entire address book. Anyway, it's better to say 'no' now rather than end up regretting saying 'yes'. Just explain that you have to be especially careful about your web profile because of your job.

38. Headhunters

To accelerate your career growth, cultivate good relationships with the top recruiters.

Your professional network is incomplete without a headhunter or two that knows the plum jobs in your sector.

It's a bit like finding a new home: that perfect job never seems to be available at the right time. You may not have time to look around for yourself but there are headhunters looking for the right candidate on behalf of their corporate clients. In the 'war for talent', they are working to fill some of the least advertised jobs, moving top performers around from one job to another when they are ready for their next career step.

Get inside the mind of the top recruiters
At the elite end of the market, international search companies operate a highly sophisticated service to fill senior appointments. They aim at matching companies and candidates for a marriage made in heaven. Their subjective judgement – do you look and sound suitable – weighs equally with your objective skills and qualifications.

They work on a confidential basis, especially if an appointment is connected to a new market initiative, though news often leaks through the 'grapevine'. One high-powered head of an exclusive London-based search firm has her own regular table at a famous West End eaterie; being seen there with her is enough to set the City rumour mill into overdrive.

An assignment can take up to three or four months and cost the client a third of the appointee's annual salary. Typically, headhunters will set out to find twenty or thirty candidates, take up references, vet them all at interview and whittle them down to a shortlist of two or three to present to their client. Top headhunters source their candidates largely through networking and contact building, often calling clandestinely to ask people for a recommendation

They're coming under pressure
Intense competition has cut the cost of recruitment dramatically and the internet has speeded up the process. As well as receiving incoming CVs via their websites, search companies work proactively to find candidates, using job boards like Monster.com, CareerBuilder and SkillsMarket. These, in turn, set out to capture pole position in specific industry sectors, so that they become a 'must see' site for people on the move.

Be on their radar
So, it's not enough to be the best person for the job with a strong track record in your field. The right people have to know about you, too. That's why you should network regularly, as a matter of routine, so that your reputation precedes you and people in your sector will mention your name favourably when the headhunter calls.

> *Here's an idea for you…*
>
> Give the headhunters a helping hand. As the job market goes global, it's harder for them to spot the talent and many have started to use web-based job boards to help with their initial trawl. So, this is another opportunity to make sure your name comes up in a preliminary web search. Do your homework on the sites that will do you most good: sector specialists; alumni associations for schools and colleges; professional associations. Then polish up that CV and upload.

The easy way out for search firms is to restrict the search to candidates already established in their careers and poach from their client's main rivals. They may be a bit sniffy about people at the beginning of their careers. However, they like to tell their clients that they work on the basis that 'if you're good, we'll find you'. Hence, the sooner you make a connection with a headhunter or search firm the better.

That first break is the vital one – once you're known, you're part of the job merry-go-round. It helps to cultivate a firm that's hungry for business and needs fresh, strong candidates. You will be tempted to cold-call a headhunter or two yourself to get the ball rolling. However, this is definitely a situation where being seen to be in demand is a huge advantage, so show a little restraint. That means you will have to rely mainly on your networking buddies to do you a big favour and mention your name and give you a glowing report. They'll be more inclined to oblige if they know they can rely on you to do the same for them in similar circumstances.

> You should nurture your headhunter because... if your ideal job comes along, they will tell you about it. Busy people don't have the time to look around for themselves.

Dianne Thompson, Chief Executive, Camelot, Lottery organisers

Idea 38 – **Headhunters**

How did it go?

Q. No one will mention my name if a headhunter calls to ask for a recommendation; hardly anyone outside the company knows of me or my work. Any suggestions?

A. If you want to get noticed by headhunters, you have to find time to do your own PR, as well as regular networking. One thing that can really raise your profile is an occasional article published in a trade publication with your name on it, as this will also be picked up in a web search. Aim for a title that people within your sector read regularly. Show some initiative in this direction at work and see if your boss will make it part of your job description to produce regular contributions.

Q. I haven't heard from a search firm since they found me my current position. What should I do to keep myself in their minds for another move when I'm ready for it?

A. Don't rely on them keeping in touch with your progress – it's an unusual search firm that thinks of you unless they have an assignment to fill. Their staff move on, too. So, once you have made a good contact, keep in touch. Send a copy of anything that reminds them of your upward mobility (e.g. an announcement of a promotion or success with a project or business deal).

39. International relations

In an increasingly globalised business world, you'll need these hot tips for networking abroad.

Cultural differences can really affect the way business is done. Here's how to go local when you're on an international business trip.

You're all excited that you're being sent on a fact-finding mission overseas. Then reality hits – there's a lot to get your head around when it comes to other cultures.

Take the handshake: Americans like 'em firm; Brits like them gentle; in Saudi Arabia they are usually accompanied by a kiss, even for men. In the West, averted eyes are a sign of insecurity or shiftiness while in the East they are a sign of respect.

If possible, take advice on the etiquette and customs of doing business from someone who has worked in the country you plan to visit. Of course, there's no way you'll get to grips with every little nuance and people do make allowances for visitors. Nevertheless, it's important to prepare yourself thoroughly to avoid any major *faux-pas*.

Idea 39 – *International relations*

Working with an interpreter

It may seem obvious, but if you don't speak the local language, you'll need to hire an interpreter. Try to meet them in advance so by the time you have your first meeting, they are comfortable with the way you speak. Let them know the issues you'll be discussing and what you hope to achieve.

At a meeting, speak to your new business contact – not the interpreter. Ask your interpreter to translate short bursts rather than long passages. Apologise for your inability to speak their language.

Ask for feedback to be certain your contact has understood your proposition – using visuals can be an enormous help. In the meeting, don't say anything that you don't want your contact to hear – they might not feel confident speaking English but they may understand it.

Dining abroad matters

The French like long lunches while Americans like to keep business lunches short and sweet. The time for main meals can vary significantly from country to country, too. Mexicans, for example, prefer something substantial mid-afternoon. Some dishes you may avoid eating at home, such as offal, are a delicacy in other places. Try not to insult your hosts and eat what you are served. Experienced travellers strongly advise that you don't ask what you're eating in case you don't like what you hear. Just cut up the food finely and pretend it's something you like.

Here's an idea for you...

Take nothing for granted – even in your own country. What passes for normal behaviour for busy townies isn't necessarily acceptable in the countryside. City business folk looking to downsize, take heed. Slow right down and develop more patience. People in rural parts will usually expect to get to know you better before doing business with you. To make a success of country living, you're going to have to learn to spend lots more time with people.

173

Gift giving

Gifts for your hosts are always a nice touch, but in some Asian countries, like Japan, they are a customary part of doing business. The Japanese don't tend to like surprise gifts so let them know in advance that you are planning to give them a present. They appreciate imported gifts such as fine liquor, collectibles and luxury brands. Expect the recipient to decline your gift out of politeness at first, then accept it later. If a Japanese contact gives you a present, you should do the same.

Special tips for women doing business abroad

In many places, businesswomen are still something of a novelty. Make sure your hosts realise it's a woman visiting so they're not caught off-guard. You may need to take a chaperone to some Far Eastern nations. In male-dominated societies, ask for the meeting room door to be kept open to avoid any suggestion of impropriety.

Most women know they'll need to cover up in Muslim nations. Also be aware trousers are a 'no-no' for businesswomen in some countries, like Thailand.

In many countries girls don't go out drinking. This can present a problem in countries like Russia, where bonding over a drink is part of the business culture. Take a maximum of two drinks then ask someone reliable to take you back the hotel.

> *The world is my country, all mankind are my brethren, and to do good is my religion.*

Thomas Paine, eighteenth-century American politician and philosopher

Idea 39 – **International relations**

How did it go?

Q. I sometimes have to talk to customers who speak English as a second language. Any tips so I don't come across as patronising?

A. Typical advice for talking to someone whose first language isn't English goes like this: speak slowly and clearly; enunciate everything you say; keep the words and sentence structure simple; and talk a little louder than usual. However, many people are so anxious to be understood they go completely over the top and end up sounding like a ham actor. As with any conversation the key is really to be yourself. Just moderate what you say according to the person's level of fluency. Ask simple questions. Avoid word play, slang and acronyms. Don't be vague or change the topic abruptly. Above all use a normal speaking voice.

Q. I will be visiting a client and hope to use my French. Can you offer some advice on doing business in a foreign language?

A. Before your visit, think about any special expressions or technical terms you might need to use. Then familiarise yourself with their foreign language equivalent. During discussions try to speak as clearly as possible. Make plenty of eye contact and use gestures. Let the other people know when you cannot comprehend what they said. It's a really good idea to jot down any figures you want to discuss to make sure everyone accurately understands them. Afterwards confirm what was said in writing to avoid any confusion.

40. Hosts with the most

Your business needs to get creative about corporate networking. Here are the latest trends.

A round of golf or a outing to the rugby is no longer enough to reward your staff for their efforts. The traditional corporate circuit of horses, boats and tennis won't woo your clients.

Cater for the growing influence of women
The gender balance in business is changing as more women climb the corporate ladder and more female entrepreneurs make their mark. By 2020, according to Barclay's Wealth, more than half the millionaires in the UK will be women. Career women are growing bored with talks on the 'glass ceiling', the invisible barrier to promotion that is said to hold them back. They are looking for new kinds of networking events designed for them – usually by other women. A catwalk show at a fashion event provides a little glitz and glamour. A visit to a spa peps up the staff outings – you'd be surprised how popular they are with the guys, too.

Coutts, a private bank that traditionally caters to the great and the good, has started to sponsor designer shows at London's Design Museum. They slant their guest list towards wealthy female entrepreneurs, who they see as a growing customer base for their services.

Say something about your brand

Coutts' initiative is an example of an attempt to change a company's stuffy image in order to attract a new segment of the market. It's always important to reinforce your core brand values. For example, Coutts is perceived to offer a high level of service on an individual basis. It would be a mistake for them to dilute this aspect of their brand by sponsoring a highly accessible event, like London Fashion Week, for example.

Present a civilised face to the world

An interest in art says something about the way your company wants to do business. Stephen Somerville of the BBC's *Antiques Roadshow* team observes that art gives people something to talk about apart from business. 'They are looking for something more tactile, more tangible,' he says. 'They have a desperate need to soak up art. They want a contrast in their lives – a civilising factor.'

> **Here's an idea for you...**
>
> Think about your clients' preferences. Make your invitations for two and show that you understand that some professionals are so much in demand they prefer events where they can spend some quality time with their spouses. Take London's Chelsea Flower Show, one of the hottest tickets in town every summer. What brings all those CEOs along? The displays of rose bushes and award-winning garden designs? No, the reason is that the companies that host them have the foresight to invite spouses too.

AT Kearney, the management consultancy company, hosts an annual corporate event at the company offices in London's Berkeley Square. They showcase the work of artists selected from the Royal Academy summer exhibitions. According to one of the company's directors, the event delivers a commercial benefit as well as encouraging the artistic community. 'It lets us put on events for people to come and visit us in our office,' he says. 'It's one of the few things you can invite clients to that their spouses are also willing to attend. It's just a nice casual atmosphere. Commercially, it's nice. Socially, it's wonderful.'

Keep in touch with your alumni

If satisfied clients are your business's future, your own people are its best ambassadors. Disgruntled ex-employees can undermine a company's reputation but 'old boys' that remain on good terms can enhance the brand and themselves can become clients. That's the experience of McKinsey & Co, the management consultancy company, whose alumni go on to influential roles in public service and every sector of industry. Their alumni network has become the gold standard for the professional services sector.

You may not have the resources to match them but you can learn from their experience. McKinsey's network provides a directory so that members of staff, past and present, can keep in touch with each other. There is the latest news from inside the company, job vacancies and software tools so you can manage your finances, like your pension account. The network links them together and has made the company an institution, strengthening its reputation and opening doors to new prospects.

Sow good services; sweet remembrances will grow them. Madame de Staël, eighteenth-century French literary figure

Idea 40 – **Hosts with the most**

How did it go?

Q. We're a small company and can't justify paying a production specialist to run events for us, but it's tough to come up with good ideas ourselves. Is there another way?

A. Loosen up! Get everyone to brainstorm ideas – welcome every suggestion, however off-the-wall, and make it clear there are no wrong answers. Think about your customers and where you're trying to take your brand. Try bringing in a creative person who can facilitate a session or two where you spark ideas off one another. For example, a kitchen design company brought in an artist who encouraged staff to paint or model new designs; they held a client evening to show off their work and got lots of useful feedback.

Q. We have a corporate intranet that keeps current staff informed. But we take loyalty seriously. Doesn't the idea of an alumni network make the decision to leave all a bit too easy?

A. Certainly if you make leaving too pleasant you risk building an organisation where people flit in and out in response to fleeting opportunities. However, if you get a reputation for cursing all who leave, potential recruits will be wary of joining in the first place; and ditherers might stay rather than pluck up the courage to leave. It's all going to depend on the type of culture you're building. Obviously you're not about to allow people access to sensitive or competitive information.

Networking

41. An affair to remember

Weddings, christenings and bar mitzvahs – there's nothing like celebrations for breaking the ice.

The charged atmosphere that surrounds a ceremony produces an enhanced opportunity to meet and bond.

Hands up if you met your current partner or spouse at a friend's wedding. So many couples say they met that way. It gives a clue to the essence of encounters at social events. Ceremonies generate a mixture of expectation and formality, which combine to produce a charged atmosphere in which people have many chances to meet and bond, often at warp speed.

Guests are primed to be on their best behaviour in public. A display of good manners has a habit of bringing out the best in people. Politeness might lurch over into something more than a superficial connection, such as a phone number, date or even a business opportunity.

Fit in and put others at their ease

To take advantage of these occasions, you must fit in. Make sure you look smart. If you don't look the part, it looks like you are not really taking the occasion to heart.

Notice what's going on around you. Start with the basics: smile, say 'please' and 'thank you' at the appropriate time. Be friendly and considerate.

Networking

Here's an idea for you...

We all like hearing positive things about ourselves, yet it is surprising how many of us have trouble accepting compliments. Say 'congratulations on your news' or even 'you look terrific today' to some people and it's not unusual to receive a distinctly frosty or even a downright rude reply. If someone praises you, don't squirm and pretend to be unworthy of their praise or put them right on a detail. Just say 'thank you' graciously. Then add a remark that allows the conversation to carry on.

If you are shy, try this little trick. Just imagine that you are not a guest at this event but one of the hosts. Look after people – introduce yourself and anyone you recognise. Bring newcomers into the conversation.

Pick up on the atmosphere. You are at a public event and your reputation is at stake, so err on the side of politeness. But gauge the mood of the moment and don't be afraid to follow your instincts if, for example, you judge that a little flirting or mildly outrageous behaviour is in keeping with the spirit of the event. Don't feel you have to be miserable at a funeral but be especially sensitive to the feelings of the bereaved; be prepared to listen attentively if they want to reminisce.

When in doubt, take your cue from other guests and mirror their behaviour. A ready smile will see you through most awkward situations.

Widen your circle
Mingle politely and make an effort to talk to as many people as possible – you don't know who you might meet. You might find yourself congregating in groups of people you know. Break away from time to time and join a new group – just hover nearby until someone brings you into the conversation. At a wedding, you all have the bride and groom as a focus so it's easy to step forward, introduce yourself and ask others about their connection. Now you can apply all your networking skills – see how far they can take you.

Greetings and goodbyes

A few key moments often determine lasting impressions. At a first meeting, for example, someone has to take the initiative on whether to shake hands or kiss. Factors like age, situation and status set different expectations. The easy way out is to follow the lead of the other party. Allow them to take charge. Be alert to their body language and mirror their behaviour precisely.

Greetings and goodbyes with a kiss ought to be a delicate and graceful affair but can turn into a bit of a nightmare if you don't handle them nicely. So much depends on the attitude and intentions of the other party.

If they want to kiss, it would be rude not to join in. Place a hand gently on a shoulder and aim for their right cheek but be prepared to switch to the other cheek right up to the last moment. Now here's the tricky bit: is it a one or two cheek job (or even more complicated)? Be decisive. If you're only going for a single peck, step in, plant a light kiss and step out. Make it obvious so the other party is not left kissing thin air.

Eighty percent of success is showing up.

Woody Allen, American director and comedian

How did it go?

Q. Is it disrespectful to talk business at a funeral?

A. It's plain to even the crassest individual that commercial opportunities are the last thing you should be thinking about when you attend funerals. However, it's perfectly natural to reminisce after the service about the deceased and their achievements. If that involves 'talking shop' (say, because the deceased ran a business, loved their work and was proud of the company they founded), then that's only being thoughtful. If that leads to a new connection with someone, that's great. You should, however, leave the nitty-gritty and deal making to another occasion.

Q. I've only just met this girl at a party and she's pouring out her life story. I feel sorry for her but it's too much too soon. How should I handle it?

A. Occasionally you come across people – usually on long plane trips – who are looking for a captive audience. Without even making a perfunctory attempt to get to know you, they launch into the intimate details of their lives as if you are a best friend or a shoulder to cry on. You may be sympathetic but don't get trapped into playing therapist. Complete strangers who share confidences so readily are rarely interested in a mutual relationship. If you think this girl is just using you as a receptacle for her emotional turmoil, wrap up the conversation now. It may be good for her but it certainly isn't good for you.

42. Your other half

As high flyers and diplomats know so well, your spouse or partner could be one of the greatest networking assets you possess.

Your other half can really help you to get the most out of social events by building closer ties with contacts and co-hosting when you entertain for business.

There's nothing like walking into a room with a special someone beside you on whom you can rely totally. Your spirits soar; you feel calmer, more confident, in control and ready to charm. The reason is trust. It is an essential part of making things work. According to a recent survey, business leaders prize the quality of trust more than expertise or experience. The person you choose to spend your life with is possibly your greatest champion and ally. This is why the survey also found that nearly two-thirds of successful company directors admit they naturally turn to their other halves when they need help.

These successful men and women rely on their partners or spouses to take some of the hard work out of networking. They can count on their other halves to talk them up whenever they can, without sounding unnatural or gushy. When they attend company 'dos' as a couple, their other half warms up potential contacts on their behalf. They might try to humour a difficult client or rescue their partner from a bore so they are free to talk to the right people.

Parents, brothers and sisters, even your kids can be useful allies when it comes to making and keeping contacts. Sir Terence Conran, founder of Habitat and a successful restaurateur, acknowledges the value of the support he's received over the years from his sister Priscilla, who created the Italian café chain Carluccio's together with her husband Antonio Carluccio.

Pairing off

One of the most important ways they help is by mingling with other 'other halves', putting them at their ease. As a result, their spouse or partner has more time to focus on business. And finally they never demand attention when their other half's mind is on the job at hand.

Most probably your spouse or partner has a distinctly different skill set to your own. Use it to the full. For example, if your other half is better at reading people and judging character, ask for their post-match analysis on any event you attend together. You can check with them if somebody really did behave as inappropriately or unreasonably as you thought – and ask their advice on the best way to react.

Here's an idea for you...

Finally, don't take your other half's efforts for granted. You would naturally acknowledge a good turn from a colleague or a business contact, so do the same for your partner. It's really important you reward them for all the time and work they have put in on your behalf. Say 'thank you' with a much-desired gift; take them out for a meal at their favourite restaurant; and, above all, be there with 100% support when it's an occasion that really matters to them.

Idea 42 – **Your other half**

Perhaps your spouse is a more natural schmoozer. With their help you can discover interests in common with your contacts, an invaluable advantage to your career or business. Or, let's say your partner is more *au courant* with the arts or sports than you – get them to fill you in before a corporate fund-raiser at a museum or attending a football game with a client.

Tight briefs

Communication is key to this teamwork. High flyers and their spouses often talk strategy before an upcoming business function. In the days running up to the next event to which you have been invited to bring a guest, brief your partner thoroughly. You should of course:

- tell them what kind of event it is – whether it's a barbecue or a formal dinner or a get-together with a client or contact
- give your other half an idea of how they're expected to dress
- tell them who'll be there and what you know about them; let them know who you want them to network with and why
- let them know what you hope to achieve.

Just as importantly, make sure your spouse or partner knows what NOT to say, for example confidential business issues they should avoid discussing.

Man's best possession is a sympathetic wife.
Euripides, Ancient Greek dramatist

How did it go?

Q. He doesn't really mean any harm but my boyfriend is an outrageous flirt and sometimes he makes me feel uncomfortable when he meets women at my work events. Any suggestions?

A. We've all been at corporate 'dos' where a colleague's significant other has created a lot of 'tut-tutting'. Maybe they came on strong to the boss's husband, goosed a junior colleague, made sexual innuendoes or dressed like a dominatrix. At the time, it's best to ignore this behaviour unless it's really embarrassing, in which case, intervene gently. This is not the time to try to sort out this particular relationship issue. However, before you invite him to the next big occasion, talk to him about why he makes you feel uncomfortable. Explain how his flirtatious ways are inappropriate, even potentially damaging to your career. If he'll make a determined effort to tone it down for your sake then bring him along.

Q. My ex and I had an ugly split last year. Now we're both attending the same conference. How do I handle the situation?

A. Forewarned, the inevitable meeting won't come as a shock and you can practice how you're going to react. Don't let any unresolved anger get the better of you. You must be polite and say 'hello', at least briefly. Think positive thoughts even if you don't feel like it. If you are on your best behaviour, the chances are that your ex will be, too. Remember you are there to meet new people not pick over the bones of a dead relationship.

43. They're going to find out who's naughty or nice

It's an old cliché, but how you behave at the office Christmas party could help or hinder you for the rest of the year.

The Christmas party is the ideal environment to open up new career possibilities. Moderation is the name of the game if you want to make the most of what is the biggest occasion on the corporate social calendar.

The pressure is on – mixing business and pleasure is always a delicate balancing act between having a good time and maintaining a professional gloss. What happens at a friend's blow-out is no big deal. What happens at a work 'do' can derail your career. It is good to celebrate the season with colleagues but treat the party like the business event it is and you won't go wrong.

Holiday finery
Even if the party is supposed to be casual don't just pull on any old thing and head for the venue. Make an effort to shine. Dressing up is strategically smart: it'll

> ### Here's an idea for you...
>
> Freelancers often get overlooked when the invitations go out for the annual Christmas bash. If you're self-employed, you've got to make doubly sure you participate in the merry-making. The holiday season is just too important a networking opportunity to miss. Not on your employers' guest list? Throw your own fun Yuletide gathering instead. Invite all your contacts and friends from the businesses who employ you. That way they'll think of you when they're commissioning more work.

help you get noticed by the right people, from senior managers to guests, like that attractive solicitor. But make sure you don't indulge in too much of a good thing. People in reindeer sweaters and bauble earrings aren't taken seriously. Plunging necklines and micro-minis will only get the office gossips working overtime.

'Plus guest'

If partners are invited, don't stick together like glue but don't ignore them completely either or you'll hear about it later. As soon as you arrive, introduce your other half to people you already know. Try to spark a conversation around a common interest so they all have lots to chat about. Then go off on your social rounds. Be sure, though, to check in occasionally to see if they're okay. And remember that public displays of passion make others squirm, so don't indulge in them and use given (rather than pet) names.

Mingling and mistletoe

Socialise tactically. The Christmas party is the ideal environment to make contacts, get colleagues onside and open up new possibilities. Introduce yourself to the financial director. If you and a team-mate haven't always seen eye to eye, why not try to improve your relationship by getting to know him a little better? Ask him about himself and his interests rather than work issues. Talk to your manager about what direction the business is heading in next year. If there's a forthcoming project that strikes your fancy, now is the time to register your interest.

All flirting must be very low profile. Risqué behaviour is the other great source of notorious stories from Christmas parties. If there's any kissing to be done, make it at home. Don't be seen talking too intimately with your married boss. No leaving with the manager from marketing that you just met. And any dancing on tables is likely to be recorded on a cell phone and played back the next day for all those who missed it.

Glad tidings of good cheer
You have been warned: the overwhelming majority of Christmas party horror stories tend to involve alcohol. So take extra care not to drink too much at holiday events. Decide on your limit and stick to it. Alternate alcohol and soft drinks. Switch to water the minute you feel a slight buzz coming on. Or maybe even give the booze a miss altogether. Appearing drunk is not a good career move. You don't want any alcohol fuelled antics to haunt you in the future.

The next day
On a final note, the next day is equally important so it's never a good idea to be the last to leave. Staggering into the office late or hungover won't go unnoticed. Taking a sick day is an even worse crime. So, make an extra effort to be punctual and full of beans the following morning.

> An office party gives you the opportunity to celebrate ... with your co-workers. You should have fun, but be careful about having too good a time. Dawn Rosenberg McKay, writer on career planning

Networking

How did it go?

Q. I've had a good time, made some new contacts and I'm ready to leave, but the party is still in full swing. How do I slip away?

A. You just want to leave quietly, having dropped in briefly to fulfil your quota of face time. However, don't try to exit unnoticed – it's rude. You must make sure that you thank the host. At office Christmas celebrations, that usually means the most senior person present. Compliment them on something you particularly enjoyed about the party. Say goodbye to everyone in the room if the party is small. Otherwise, acknowledge the people you talked to. Obviously you should be as brief as possible so the other guests can get back to the party as soon as possible.

Q. One of my workmates is becoming a bit too frisky for my liking under the influence of alcohol and mistletoe. He's starting to annoy me. How can I get rid of him?

A. The festive high spirits may have ignited this man's lust but just because it's a party doesn't mean you have to laugh off his unwanted behaviour. If someone is coming on too strong, tell him he is making you feel uncomfortable. Be calm and firm but not nasty. If he persists, signal to a close colleague for help. Before the end of the evening arrange for someone you trust to see you safely to your door.

44. High-octane networking

What it takes to mix it with the big movers and shakers.

The rich and powerful network among themselves pretty much like the rest of us — on issues that matter to them. It's just that the scale of their issues is a tad more breathtaking than most.

Not convinced? Then get yourself invited to Davos, Switzerland next January to attend the World Economic Forum, an annual summit for a thousand of the world's leading business people and assorted members of the great and the good.

Fly in for the whole five days or touch down for a few hours – as long as your whirlwind schedule allows. There's a set agenda for each day of the event, a programme designed to tackle the hottest economic and social issues of the day, but the real connections are made at the coffee breaks and social engagements that fill every waking hour of the day and most of the night.

If you are exceedingly important, Bill Gates may invite you for a nightcap at the Fluella Restaurant on the last night. An invitation to Booz Allen & Hamilton's late night party is slightly less prestigious but is not to be sniffed at, featuring as it does 'cheese and chocolate and wine and whiskey and music and more'.

Networking

> **Here's an idea for you...**
>
> Conduct your next meeting standing up. Studies show that conversations between people who are standing are significantly shorter than those between people who are sitting down. People perceive a person standing up at a meeting to have higher status than those who sit. Decisions tend to be quicker and meeting times shorter, a huge cost saving in terms of people's time, especially if expensive lawyers and bankers are charging by the hour.

When it's all over you fly out, having found that the ultra-influential do much the same as networkers everywhere: they talk too much, sleep too little and eat too many things on sticks. And, yes, they do give out business cards and collect other people's contact details in a BlackBerry or Rolodex.

A difference of scale

Like everyone else, the rich and influential are more than happy to meet others like themselves. They discuss their plans and problems; they discover – to their relief – that they are not, after all, the only ones struggling with a particular issue; and they rejoice when they find a like-minded soulmate, who might support them in their endeavours. They can float their latest venture or look out for their next career move. Their issues are surprisingly similar to other networkers, give or take a few zeros on the pay cheque.

The rich, like the rest of us, like to talk to other people who understand what matters to them, such as looking after their family's future. They're interested in finding ways to boost investment returns or reduce the impact of tax changes on their wealth. They compare fees they pay lawyers and percentages that private bankers charge them for their services, like running a 'family office', to handle their investment portfolios.

Private banks organise events where high-net-worth individuals can come together. Sometimes they organise sessions in tiers, according to the wealth of participants: someone with $5 million to invest is less likely to be looking at the riskier end of the spectrum, like a venture capital investment, than someone with $50 million. They generally exclude financial services professionals – other than invited speakers – who might try to buttonhole members.

Jobs worth a lot
When it comes to changing jobs, networking looms even larger in the lives of those at the very highest levels.

The web has eaten away the tail end of the 'old boys' network' that used to fill the top jobs. More than half those earning up to $500,000 a year say that they would be 'very likely' to post their CV on an internet job board. Headhunters now routinely use social networking sites to check out potential candidates and their friends.

But those on $1 million a year or more are much more reserved about job hunting. Few would be likely to search out any form of advert when they are looking for a job, either online or in print. They are more likely to sit back and wait for the headhunters to come calling. Or they could send a whisper around the grapevine. A quiet word with a network buddy will take care of that – possibly during one of those coffee breaks at Davos.

Wealth preservation is our primary focus, but the importance of family is something beyond measure. Mark Peters, High Net Worth Group, Citigroup Private Bank

How did it go?

Q. I've been working my way steadily up the career ladder. How can I leap-frog the competition and catapult myself into the stratosphere?

A. There's an outside chance that joining the right club might do the trick. London clubs like the Groucho, Hospital and Soho House provide relaxed and informal surroundings for 'creative entrepreneurs'. They provide a heady mixture of social activity and networking for high-rollers working in creative fields like music, technology and the arts. A creative spark might just bridge the gap between an ambitious type looking for an opportunity and a corporate type looking for young talent.

Q. Okay, I still need convincing that the ultra-wealthy network the same way as the rest of us. Just how do I get myself on the guest list for events like Davos?

A. You can't usually ask for an invitation directly but a word from a recent delegate to one of the programme organisers could open the door for you if you have something truly outstanding to contribute. Approach it in the same way you would make any new high-level contact. For example, if you were to cold-call someone like Bill Gates he's probably going to say 'no', but if you can get an introduction to someone who he admires and respects through your own network, he might just say, 'tell me more about this new guy'.

Idea 44 – **High-octane networking**

45. Networking craft

There are well-tried techniques that can take you beyond the superficial information available from company websites and marketing brochures.

Use our insider tips to establish rapport and pick up the latest news on your competitors or a prospective employer.

Today, there's more information available than ever – but so much of it actually tells you very little. You have to dig deeper to go beyond the corporate announcements. However, most people's knee-jerk reaction to a stranger's enquiry is to deal with it as fast as possible so they can get on with their work. The simple way to do that without actually being rude is to give out a little information. They'll take any path that makes their job easier.

On a cold-call, you could fall at the first hurdle if they ask whether you have checked out their website and you have to admit that you haven't. So, do your homework before you pick up the phone. If you can, avoid the call centre number and aim for a contact in a customer-facing function like PR or sales and marketing, where you can expect to talk to someone who is used to dealing with new enquiries.

Pass the interrogation test

It's surprising how much information you can gather on your first call to a company if you go about it the right way. Treat whoever answers the phone as an individual

– not just someone who is there to take your call. Avoid wasting their time but see if you can establish a rapport with them. Find your own preferred calling style (be it standing, smiling, dressing up), one that best allows your natural warmth and enthusiasm to come through in your voice.

Start with a question that your contact will find easy to answer. For example, check that you have got through to the company location you expected. If you are trying to find out the name of a decision-maker – for example, a marketing manager – say something along the lines of: 'I'm dropping a line to whoever takes care of your marketing; can you tell me who that is?'

Once you succeed in finding someone to help you, make the most of it. Tell them you want to set up a meeting with the marketing manager. Use a question that gives them an easy choice rather than a decision to make: ask if it's best to call direct or send an email. Then check that you have all the contact information you need, like email addresses and the company's correct postal address.

Intelligence gathering

Events like conferences and exhibitions are a perfect place to meet people and make contacts but can offer slim pickings when it comes to real knowledge about your competitor's plans or a prospective employer. The corporate quality control function prevents you learning anything that a company does not want you to know.

> **Here's an idea for you...**
>
> Nodding pays. In face-to-face conversation, show your approval by nodding enthusiastically – it will keep them talking. Research has shown the most effective nodding is a sequence of three successive nods at regular intervals. Fast nodding indicates to the speaker that you are waiting to speak yourself and have heard enough. Slow nodding expresses interest. Make it a deliberate group of three at a steady pace and you'll maximise interaction.

Networking

Always collect a copy of the delegate list at a conference or exhibition. Take a look to see if you recognise any names so you are ready to offer a warm greeting if you bump into someone you know. Make a mental note of the names of people that you would like to meet so you can play spot-the-name on the badge during the coffee break.

Press conferences are a better bet for insider information. They are, of course, intended for corporate announcements but the organiser – usually a PR agency or adviser – knows that if they are to attract a decent turnout from the press, their client has to raise the corporate skirts at least a little and will advise them accordingly.

Stick to events where the chief executive will hold the floor; they do at least know what's going on and are often quite candid in their views. Now and again, their passion leads them to reveal more than they intended. They are also the most likely to escape the censorship that applies to other members of the management team.

In your thirst for knowledge, be sure not to drown in all the information.

Anthony J. D'Angelo, author *The College Blue Book*

How did it go?

Q. I don't like to put people under pressure by asking them intrusive questions. Won't they end up disliking me if I do?

A. Perhaps surprisingly, most people will forgive someone being demanding as long as they are polite and professional. They realise that you have a job to do and appreciate your determination. There's nothing wrong with being slightly cheeky, either, once you have established a degree of rapport with someone; for example, by suggesting a solution that gets the job done faster. Just don't overdo it and remember to show respect at all times.

Q. I quite often meet new contacts but come away having learnt very little. How do I get people talking?

A. Practise the techniques of gently probing for further information. If you want a simple 'no' or 'yes' answer, ask a closed question, such as: 'Are you planning to set up a production facility in China?' This type of question is a good way to control a conversation. If you want to get someone to open up to you, ask open questions, such as: 'What are your plans for overseas expansion?' This type of question generally elicits more information and is good for building rapport. Eventually, you can learn to switch people's conversation on and off like a tap.

46. Psst … don't pass it on

Skilled networkers follow the rules for handling gossip and innuendo.

Go ahead and gossip — its okay. You just need to learn how to tread the fine line between sharing the low-down and genuine indiscretion.

Do you like nothing better than a good gossip? Don't feel guilty. Contrary to all those rumours spread by po-faced people, everyone is at it. It's human nature to want to chat about what you and others are doing. At its best, gossip is a delightfully delicious exchange of information, which helps you bond with others. It's a prime networking tool if ever there was one. But just like champagne, gossip is highly intoxicating and can suddenly go to your head. So, you need to be aware of the dangerous pitfalls.

Keep secrets secret

When someone you know asks you to keep some commercial or personal news under wraps, you should respect their confidence. Equally, when people open up to you or share intimate personal details, what they say is strictly for your ears only. Fight the temptation to pass on anything you learn to another party. If you are overburdened with a particularly juicy scoop and you really cannot resist getting it off your chest, make sure you tell someone completely out of the loop. Otherwise the story will spread like wildfire and somebody will trace its origins right back to you.

Deconstruct what you hear

Don't just digest a tasty communiqué unquestioningly. Learn to read between the lines. Many a tale has been watered down or altered on its trip around the grapevine. Think first and do some digging around if necessary. Is your source unimpeachable? Have they put their own spin on the gossip? Mischief-making often comes from a mixture of bitterness, jealousy and spite. If you have ever had malicious rumours spread about you, it may be a comfort to know that manipulative individuals who twist tales or deceive usually get caught out. They soon develop a reputation for untrustworthiness.

Email on the record

Discretion is a must. It is all too easy for your IT department and work colleagues to access your email box. Never put in writing something you wouldn't say to someone's face. Train yourself to double-check addresses so your dispatch does not end up in the wrong hands. Never use your work address to send confidential information to outside contacts and friends; use a personal address. You should immediately delete any message you receive that contains red-hot gossip.

> **Here's an idea for you...**
>
> Use your talent for gossip to spread positive news. Pass on information that makes other people look good. Smart gossips never take credit for other people's achievements. Instead they give credit where it is due and compliment others on a job well done. When others seek to look important and successful they'll help them create the right impression. In return people speak well of them out of loyalty, so they look good too.

Try not to be overheard

There's always a risk that you will be overheard when you gossip. Before you get too involved in a really good exchange, take a look around you. You never know who could be eavesdropping on your little chit-chat. Keep your voice low and talk with caution – especially in the office. Remember that gestures and facial expressions speak volumes too.

If you think you've been caught in the act, try to recall what you said. As long as it wasn't anything indiscreet, don't apologise because it will only magnify the incident. However, if you have been overheard speculating or spreading scandal you have some very serious grovelling to do.

Handling gossip about you

If you overhear a conversation about you, alert the speakers to your presence. Rise above the temptation to continue listening in and catch them putting you down. It will only make the situation more awkward. Keep your cool – outbursts are only more grist for the mill. Calmly confront the source of the gossip and stop the rumour mill in its tracks.

If you step over that fine line and fail to follow the rules of etiquette on handling gossip, you're heading for a harsh dressing down from friends or colleagues. In an extreme case you could fall out irrevocably with them. You could face dismissal from your job if you spread malicious rumours or pass on sensitive information about your company's financial performance.

Scandal is gossip made tedious by morality. Oscar Wilde

Idea 46 – **Psst … don't pass it on**

How did it go?

Q. I always keep my head down at the office and keep myself to myself. So why do the people I work with talk behind my back?

A. People are just as wary of those who never gossip as they are of those who spread tales continuously. Gossip is good for bonding and team building; your standoffish behaviour has alienated you from the group. They probably won't say anything in front of you because they don't trust you. If you want to know what's going on and improve your popularity rating, you're going to have to be a lot more friendly, talkative and socially active.

Q. I enjoy a good old chat with one of my workmates but she does feed me the odd line or two of flapdoodle. Is there anything I can do to curb her habit of telling me untruths?

A. You can tackle this problem in several ways. What you choose to do depends on what she's been lying about as well as how close you are. If she's not hurting anybody, you could just choose to ignore her fibs. Humour is an effective way of combating any tendency towards tall tales. You could try saying something like 'come on Pinocchio, your nose is growing' whenever she comes out with a real howler. However if you've rumbled something more sinister, you need to have a serious word in private before her lies get out of hand.

47. Staying the course

You've found the right networking groups to join. Now do your bit to keep them active and flourishing. Here's how to stop the fizz from going flat.

It takes a combination of inspiration and hard work to keep busy people engaged in a network. Aim at generating interaction between members and meeting members' needs with a highly targeted programme.

Maintain a community of interest

It's important to achieve the right mix of social and business networking activities. Find a model that works for your group, one that uniquely meets the needs of the members. For example, chief executives can find it a little lonely at the top, as the buck stops with them. Their ideal networking group would therefore offer plenty of scope for mutual support as well as management training and individual coaching. Most people like working in small groups. They find they can interact productively in groups of around half-a-dozen and collaborate to maximum effect. They can discuss their individual business problems in turn and come up with recommendations for solutions among themselves. This type of structure helps develop bonds between members, which contributes to the sustainability of the group.

We all need inspiration and role models, so think about inviting guest speakers to talk about a hot topic, something of interest to a majority of members, such as how to find good staff – and keep them. The Academy for Chief Executives (www.chiefexecutive.com) seems to have struck the right mix. It's a club for business leaders, which has more than 300 members. The club offers a range of different membership packages, but essentially members attend one day per month.

Each monthly session is divided into two. The morning session is led by a leading professional in a specialist field of knowledge, which could range from yoga to sales and marketing. The speaker encourages interaction and applies their specialist knowledge in a practical and useful way, focusing on members' issues from their business or personal life.

One member, the chief executive of a motor dealer group, points out that membership is not suitable for people who are too proud to open up to others, or who refuse to face up to a business problem that has been identified by other members. ACE's founder claims that membership, which costs a one-off fee of £350 plus a monthly subscription of £700, is more valuable than appointing a non-executive director at a comparable cost. In practice, he says, time, rather than cost, tends to be the biggest sticking point for potential members.

Connect with your contact programme
With personal contact limited by competing demands on time, the challenge for networking groups is to keep members involved between meetings. This requires a high-quality contact programme. Personalised emails deliver invitations to

Here's an idea for you...
Pick your time to call. Did you know you have a much better chance of getting hold of a contact between 8.30 and 10.00 in the morning or after 4.30 in the afternoon? At these times people are less likely to be busy with routine tasks or away from their desks at meetings. As a result they are more likely to pick up the phone because it's more convenient for them to talk.

forthcoming events. A regular newsletter brings news of members' achievements and events of interest to the community. A well-designed and frequently updated website offers 'sticky content' (i.e. content that brings members back regularly to visit the site).

One very effective form of 'sticky content' is a monthly trend report that identifies economic, technological or social trends that will affect markets in the medium to long term (e.g. 'companies measure their carbon footprints' or 'payment by mobile phone threatens credit cards'). These are of interest to people in most industries and can provide talking points for discussions on strategy and market opportunities.

Blogging to build

Communication of the 'I talk, you listen' kind doesn't keep bright people involved for long. Interaction is essential to keep lively minds engaged. The whole point about blogs is that they have to take risks to succeed. You only take notice of them and keep coming back for more if they have something distinctive to say. They only provoke you to post a comment if they ring true. The author has to be honest about themselves and their business and not be afraid to make negative comments when they are warranted. If they are an exercise in executive vanity or become stale, they go the way of sanitised corporate information, voicemails and company spam.

Perseverance is the hard work you do after you get tired of doing the hard work you already did. Newt Gingrich, American politician

How did it go?

Q. I've tried to keep in touch with colleagues I had at a previous job but after a year or two, we have all changed jobs and fallen out of touch. What's the best way to maintain the contact?

A. The main requirement is a way for all of you to communicate with each other. A website is an ideal and inexpensive solution – make sure it is secure, well-designed and maintained. Provide network members with a directory so that they can contact each other easily. Post the latest news and gossip from members, plus details of events and special occasions like anniversaries. Extra features like job vacancies and special offers bring people back to look at the site regularly, but only if they are up to date.

Q. We occasionally invite guest speakers to deliver a talk at our networking meetings – a specialist in anything from health and safety to business mentoring. How should I look after them so that they'll come back again?

A. Many professionals fulfil speaking engagements as a way to market themselves or their company and are happy to provide their services for free. Nevertheless, you should treat them as VIPs. Make sure you introduce them properly before they speak, with a brief account of their qualifications and achievements. Brief them in advance and discuss the format of the event. Cover important points such as presentation equipment and how they prefer to deal with questions from the floor.

48. Losing graciously

Sometimes we just don't get our own way. Be a good loser and you'll win another day.

Didn't get that job? Denied a pay rise? Unlucky in love? Rejection is a painful reality. It may be nothing personal but it still hurts. What's important is how you deal with it and bounce back.

'It felt like I had been kicked in the stomach,' recalls a woman who was fired, asked to clear her desk and leave the same day after working as a personal assistant to a director of an international bank. An entirely natural reaction. There's no percentage in adopting a stiff upper lip when something like this happens to you. It's healthy to acknowledge how you feel and to talk openly about it with your closest friends and allies.

Keep it real

Be honest and realistic about the situation. Look yourself in the eye and ask if your performance genuinely justified that pay rise. If you've been fired, tell people what happened. When you trip up, take responsibility for your own actions and don't point fingers at people who are not to blame. Explain what you have learnt

Idea 48 – **Losing graciously**

from the experience without going into a long rambling account. Keep it brief and above all sound positive and enthusiastic about your future.

Don't take it personally

It's hard not to, of course, especially if you have been fired. But there are plenty of reasons why you may have been fired other than your performance: it may say more about your boss's judgement or pressure within the company for cutbacks. Similarly, the reason you did not get that job could be down to bad timing or the presence of an internal candidate with an inside track. Part of the problem with these situations is that they are a reminder that you are not in charge of your own destiny quite as much as you would like. You shouldn't beat yourself up over something you have little control over.

A 'no' is as good as a 'yes' (almost)

As top sales people know, prospects reject offers, not people. When you ask for something like a job or a pay rise, the answer has to take one of three directions: 'yes', 'no' or 'maybe'. In some ways, 'maybe' is the worst response because it just leaves you in limbo. If someone rejects your pitch, it means they either don't recognise the benefits or don't value them at the moment. But at least it produced a response – now you can take your proposition elsewhere.

Here's an idea for you...

Fire your boss. Many people carry on hitting their heads against a brick wall when really they should be moving the goalposts. Don't give up something you believe in too easily, but be realistic. Accept rejection as feedback. If you are not succeeding where you are, find a new company or a new role where you can be happy. When you feel good about yourself, it shows. People connect with you more easily. Not everyone will buy what you're selling, of course, but your enthusiasm will speed your progress.

211

Learn the lessons
Before moving on, pause long enough to find out what you can about the way your boss or client made the decision. Learn any lessons that help you refine your proposition and then try your pitch on someone who will appreciate it more.

Get right back where you belong
The people that land back on their feet fastest are honest about what has happened. They pause to work out why they have been fired, say, and refocus their plans to reduce the chances of it happening again. They also rely on support from their friends and cheerleaders.

Before she cleared her desk, the fired PA sat down to write up her CV. 'I decided not to let it beat me,' she says. She was determined to get back into the job market quickly. She set up meetings with her networking contacts and interviews with agencies and search companies. She also made sure she found time for a daily workout, so that she arrived at meetings feeling invigorated, enthusiastic and positive about her future.

Good people are good because they've come to wisdom through failure.
William Saroyan, American author and playwright

Idea 48 – *Losing graciously*

How did it go?

Q. All I ever seem to get is 'maybe'. For example: 'maybe I'll help' or 'maybe I'll see you, but not now'. How do I get a 'yes' or 'no'?

A. Practise! Write down a list of people who might want what you have to offer. Use your networking skills to contact them. Push a bit more than you would normally and don't take 'maybe' for an answer. The aim is to eliminate those that won't agree to your proposition: for a reference, introduction or meeting, etc. Keep track of your progress each day as you polish up your ability to weed out the 'maybes'.

Q. I'm managing to get interviews but when I tell them I was fired from my last job, they seem to overlook me. What should I do?

A. Stay open and honest. It's usually easier finding a job when you already have one, so accept that this time will probably be tougher. Expect a potential employer to want to hear the reasons why you were fired, and expect them to want to talk to your previous boss to hear the other side of the story. Whatever you do, do not bad-mouth your previous employer, as this will set alarm bells ringing. Stick to the truth, without labouring the story. Above all, be enthusiastic and positive about the future so a potential employer can see what you have to offer.

Networking

49. Tackling cyber theft

The last thing you need is for someone else to benefit from your networking efforts. Take these simple precautions to help protect your online identity.

Once upon a time, an identity thief had to piece together information from a victim's wallet or handbag or rummage through their rubbish bins for personal documents. Now that it's a lot easier, you should take sensible precautions in your online activities.

Social network sites are a powerful way to make contacts. People with shared interests can meet and introduce each other to new ideas and other new contacts, so you appear to generate new friends at an astonishing rate.

The problem is that online networking seems such a casual affair that you tend to be far more liberal with information about yourself than you ever would be in a face-to-face situation. You know you can always log-off if something – or somebody – annoys you. This can easily seduce you into a false sense of security and false belief that there are no immediate consequences to your actions.

> **Here's an idea for you…**
>
> Do an online search for yourself. You may be surprised at how many hits you discover. Make a note of all the personal information about yourself that you find – it's best to write it down as you go. If you use any of the details you come across for identification purposes (e.g. in answer to the security questions that a bank or credit card company holds as part of the identification sequence), change them immediately.

However, there are potential hazards if you play fast and loose in the virtual world. Apart from the obvious danger of losing money to online fraudsters, identity thieves can play havoc with your good name. Malicious pranksters have already targeted some victims by repeatedly applying for credit in their name at multiple addresses, leading to a poor credit rating. How long will it be before an unscrupulous job-hunter stoops to similar levels of skulduggery and sends out spoiler CVs in the name of rival candidates to eliminate the competition?

Seeing your page on a social network site also gives old contacts a reason to get back in touch with you: ex-boyfriends and girlfriends, old school friends or just people you met at a party. Because you are online, people will assume you are fair game and that they can reintroduce themselves to your life, welcome or not.

Sites like Facebook and MySpace give users an option to block access to their profile page to everybody except invited 'friends'. However, these details are liable to leak more widely – through 'friends' of 'friends'. Many commentators also think it's only a matter of time before content like this becomes available through web search engines like Google.

Surprisingly, around 25% of users do not even restrict access to their profile page – they leave their personal information open to abuse. HSBC bank points out that the answer to many of the security questions that financial services companies ask to verify your identity are often available on a victim's profile page (e.g. a pet's name, the name of your first school or the first album you bought).

Many people also post their date of birth, home address, the name of their first school or college and work history. One survey showed that almost 90% of social network site users post their full name and 65% their email address. This makes the fraudster's task simple.

There are signs that the banks are growing increasingly reluctant to reimburse losses incurred when an ID thief runs up debts on your credit card, if you have been 'negligent', which includes careless posting on a website.

So, look before you leap and don't throw away your experience in the real world when you decide to go online.

Remember the virtue of discretion
In real life, you develop friendships gradually, among other people at work or college, say, and get to know them. However, in the virtual world, you have less of a chance to gather the clues that allow you to build up trust gradually. Until you develop that relationship of trust with someone online or with a website, always keep personal details to yourself.

Prevent fraudsters stealing your key data

All a fraudster needs to start stealing your identity is a name, address and date of birth. With these in place, the fraudster can build up all the other details that are needed to apply for a credit card (like your phone number, employment details and your mother's maiden name). These details make it all too easy to apply for copies of documents, like a birth certificate, driving license or even passport, which a fraudster needs to open a bank account in your name.

> Surfing the internet without the use of privacy control software is like having a million one-night stands without using a condom.

Sharon Lench, *PC Magazine*

*Idea 49 – **Tackling cyber theft***

How did it go?

Q. Where can I find out more about staying safe online?

A. Visit 'Get Safe Online', the website for a campaign backed by the UK government and sponsored by eBay, Microsoft and HSBC. See www.getsafeonline.org.

Q. What personal details should I keep safe?

A. Until you develop a relationship of trust with someone, avoid giving away these details and never post them on a website.

- your mother's maiden name
- where you work (it's okay to say what you do)
- name of your first school or college
- your full address, phone number and date of birth (give your age range if you want)
- your personal email address (use an alternative you've set up specially on one of the freely available internet email services such as Google, Yahoo! or Hotmail).

Q. My ex-boyfriend saw my profile online and messaged me to suggest we met up again. What should I do?

A. That really depends on why you split up. If you want to meet up with him again, fine. If you don't, reply that you appreciate the thought, but your relationship reached its natural conclusion and you don't feel it's appropriate to try to relive the past.

50. Exit strategies

Learn how to move on to new pastures without burning bridges.

The manner of your leaving can create a lasting impression with your manager and colleagues. Be classy and do the right thing — your reputation is at stake.

You're about to leave your company for a better job. You may be tempted to tell your boss what you really think of him and get those grievances off your chest. Don't. It's definitely not a good idea. However deserved your criticism may be, bad-mouthing an employer will not do your reputation any good. You should also avoid it at job interviews: potential employers may wonder what you'll say about *them* at a later date.

When you're about to move on, your main aim is to cement relationships and protect your professional reputation. Everyone you meet at work is a valuable potential member of your network.

Make that announcement
Once you have your new job offer confirmed in writing, announce your departure, unless there is a specific advantage in keeping quiet. Whatever the terms of your contract, the sooner you give notice, the sooner your company can start looking for a replacement.

Idea 50 – **Exit strategies**

Tell your line manager and deliver a resignation letter. It shouldn't say much more than that you are leaving and your last day will be … Short and sweet is best. Do not assume that your boss will pass on your news and, in any case, you want to break the news to close colleagues before they hear it from anyone else.

Make a list of people you want to tell personally. You'll naturally include those with whom you have a good working relationship; also include those who might help your future career. Don't ignore your company's top people. Chief executives often feel they are the last to hear news on the company grapevine, so make a point of telling them, if only as a matter of courtesy. Get round to each of them fast and in person if possible – but only after you have told your line manager. If you have developed 'sponsors' within your company – people whom you respect and who rate your own performance – this is the time to make a point of thanking them for the support they have given you.

> **Here's an idea for you…**
>
> If you're leaving, make life as easy as possible for whoever takes over your responsibilities. It will enhance your professional reputation. So, finish off as much of your current workload as possible. What you can't finish, you must hand over professionally. Prepare a handover document, which will bring your successor instantly up to speed. It should include a status report on unfinished business, contact information and any useful tips that will help, such as the next steps on a project.

Get the story straight

People will want to know the reason why you're leaving. If your role is high profile, think about making a call to the editor of the 'People on the move' column in the trade paper or national dailies.

Keep it short and simple: if you are on the move to a better job, talk about the challenge of a new opportunity. If you've been fired, explain that sometimes a change is in everybody's best interests.

Your company may have other ideas
Of course, if you are joining a competitor or your job involves access to privileged information, your company may want you off the premises immediately after you announce your departure. Often the problem is the other way around: while you are keen to go, they want you to stay as long as possible.

Clear the decks
Tie up all those loose ends before you leave. It's surprising how often the name of someone who has recently left a company becomes tarnished by criticism. You can't defend yourself once you have gone, so take steps to avoid unfair blame.

Update your own records
Good contacts are one of the most valuable perks of any job. Before announcing your departure, make sure your phone and address book are completely up to date with contact details for your colleagues, suppliers and customers.

Exit smiling
Take leave of your colleagues graciously. You just never know when you might meet them again or what influence they may have on your ambitions. If you change jobs within the same industry sector, you may meet them sooner than you expect.

There is nothing wrong with change, if it is in the right direction. Winston Churchill

Idea 50 – **Exit strategies**

How did it go?

Q. My HR manager, Jane, has asked me for an exit interview. I've got real concerns about my boss's integrity. How honest should I be?

A. Whatever you say in an exit interview should be in confidence but it's always wise to check the ground rules first. The idea behind the interview is to make improvements to the organisation but beware of placing Jane and yourself in a tricky position. Consider the chances that what you say will lead to decisive action – there's not much point in rocking the boat where the likelihood of remedial action is slim. Talk to friends or colleagues in advance so you can make your mind up before the interview. Whatever you decide, it's best to stick to constructive comments and concrete suggestions for improvement.

Q. It seems a bit naff to bring in a cake on my last day. Any suggestions for an alternative 'leaving do'?

A. If you're lucky, your closest colleagues will have taken up a collection for you and organised a farewell speech from your boss or a senior member of the management team. If you hear nothing on the grapevine, come up with your own farewell celebration – especially if you have been fired – as it shows you are leaving with a sense of pride. Suggest a drink after work at a nearby bar or café. Invite everyone, without exception – whatever you may feel about some colleagues, now is the time to do the right thing.

51. The home front

Neighbours can be troublesome thorns in your side or reliable buddies. Follow this guide to diplomacy on your home patch.

Show your neighbours you know how to do the right thing. If you behave responsibly, they are likely to follow your lead and tensions are unlikely to arise.

Ideally, we all want to live in a 'good neighbourhood', with well-maintained homes and clean, crime-free streets populated by friendly people who look out for one another. Yet, according to some really shocking research from a housebuilder, roughly one-third of people would cross the street to avoid their neighbours. Networking skills are a key to reversing this attitude; if you want good neighbours, you have to build – and preserve – a civilised relationship. Start by talking to them and then behave as you would in your career-building ambitions.

Go on, introduce yourself
You might feel a bit awkward but take the lead. Knock on doors and introduce yourself. It will give you a much better idea of who your neighbours are and how they live. It will also establish the fact that you are approachable, minimising any tendency towards tit-for-tat reaction should any misunderstandings occur.

Keep the noise to a minimum

Noise is the number one cause of disputes between neighbours. If you are considerate, they're more likely to be considerate in return.

- Whether you're into Bach and Mozart or house and techno, no one else in the neighbourhood should have to put up with the music on your stereo.
- Party animals should inform the neighbours about their forthcoming gatherings.
- Send Rover on a behavioural correction course if he barks constantly.
- Walls between apartments are often thin. The people next door don't share your love of *Desperate Housewives*, so don't watch television with the sound blaring.
- Indulging in piano practice in the middle of the night when you can't sleep will not endear you to neighbours.
- The tinkling of wind chimes can drive some people nuts so place them out of earshot.

Avoid offensive behaviour

To keep things on an even keel, it's important to think about how your actions will affect your neighbours. Show them the kind of respect you would like to be shown yourself and set a good example.

- Making renovation plans? Don't wait until the day the builders start work to warn your neighbours.
- Gardens are a safe place for kids to play but make sure they keep the noise to a reasonable level and don't cause any damage to the property next door.
- Issue visitors with clear instructions about where they can and cannot park their cars.
- No one appreciates being smoked out so tell the people living around you

> *Here's an idea for you...*
>
> When it's needed, always get in there first with an apology. Let's face it, moving into a new home is a messy business. There will be cartons, furniture, suitcases and sacks of rubbish everywhere. It's impossible not to get in somebody's way or crash about, especially when you're moving stuff into a flat. Nerves can fray, so it's a good idea to make a pre-emptive apology – a box of chocolates is an excellent gesture, or a bunch of flowers.

Networking

before you light a bonfire.
- Striptease and acts of a romantic nature are best performed in private with the curtains firmly drawn.
- Think before you cook in your apartment. Strong food smells lingering in the hallway aren't very popular.
- Keep your pets on the straight-and-narrow too. Don't allow Mittens to treat your neighbour's bird feeder as his own personal game reserve.

Help keep the neighbourhood looking nice

A little thought can help avoid a scruffy, run-down appearance to your neighbourhood, which can attract crime and affect property prices.
- Whether you're going on holiday or simply having a thorough clear-out, don't put rubbish sacks out before they're due for collection.
- Avoid leaving broken washing machines, old chairs and other debris outside your door for weeks on end awaiting a trip to the tip.
- Make sure the grass is kept short during the summer months.
- Trim your hedges and trees regularly. Keep exterior paintwork on doors, window frames and fences in good condition.
- Ensure builders working on your property don't dump rubble all over the place.

Whenever you're in conflict with someone, there is one factor that can make the difference between damaging your relationship and deepening it. That factor is attitude.

William James, American psychologist and philosopher

Idea 51 – **The home front**

How did it go?

Q. I've just bought my first apartment and plan to rent a room out to help cover the mortgage. Any advice?

A. Besides helping to reduce your mortgage, flat-sharing has plenty of other advantages, like good company and an increased network of friends. However, because you're living in such proximity, you have to make an even greater effort to keep relations harmonious. Try not to become territorial. Your flatmate's room is their private sanctum. Always ask before 'borrowing' their groceries or clothes. Clean up after yourself and do your share of the housework. No hogging communal facilities like the bathroom. Ask for their okay before throwing a party. Don't allow your new squeeze to take up residence without their agreement. Above all discuss any issues rather than leaving a note.

Q. The row of trees bordering my property and several of my neighbours' houses could use a good prune. Should I ask my neighbours to share the cost of cutting them back?

A. Overhanging branches are right up there with noise on the hit parade of irritants between adjoining households. Trees can cause an amazing amount of damage if allowed to grow unchecked. If the trees border everyone's property, it's reasonable to ask everyone to chip in. Even if they aren't particularly co-operative, pay to get the job done anyway; it's the responsible thing to do and otherwise you're simply storing up problems. But be sure you keep your neighbours in the loop about when the work will be carried out.

52. Boy meets girl

Top tips for boosting your chances with the opposite sex.

Finding Miss or Mister Right calls for networking skills a lot like those you need to get a promotion or a new job. It's all in the attitude. With an appealing sparkle and a proactive approach, you, too, could find a fine romance.

We all have an idea of the right partner for us in the back of our minds. They may be rich, a rock star, a sporting hero or a sensitive artistic soul. They may be witty and have long blond hair. Well, abandon these criteria now. Nobody is going to live up to your ideals. Your search for perfection is getting in the way of building meaningful relationships. Here's how to get real.

- *Get empowered with self-help books.* Sure, those self-help books can be effusive but all that optimism never hurt anyone. In fact their sunny outlook is positively infectious. They are just what you need if you feel down, suffer from the dating demons or fear rejection after a bad break-up. Reading self-help books will help boost your confidence and get you back on the track to success.
- *Stem the flow of alcohol.* Contrary to what you might think, a few extra glasses won't help you relax when you're out to meet new people. Alcohol will make

Idea 52 – **Boy meets girl**

you even more nervous and have you babbling on about nothing in particular. It clouds your judgement. You could even end up having a one-night stand that you'll regret in the cold morning light.

- *Stop obsessing over your beauty regime.* Hello, ladies, are you listening? Your weight, hair, make-up and nails don't need to be perfect in order to attract dates. There is a big difference between good grooming and high maintenance. All that dieting, toning, colouring and waxing might make you feel better about yourself but frankly men find your fixation with preening a turn-off rather then a come-on.
- *Don't travel in packs.* A big group of mates, especially all-girl or all-boy gangs, are really, really scary. Even the boldest would-be suitor will think twice before attempting to chat you up when faced with a gawking, sniggering mob. It is much easier to meet new people as a dynamic duo or a solo artist.
- *Revamp your image.* What you wear and how you wear it says a lot about you. If you're stuck in a dating rut, why not try changing your image? A fresh new look might be just what you need to radiate an alluring energy. However, avoid those revealing, over-sexy styles; you'll just appear desperate.
- *Happy hunting grounds.* If you keep running into the same old people, it's time for a change of scenery. Go somewhere different, like an ice rink or a street market. Have a drink in a wine bar or hotel lounge instead of a pub. Check out a photography exhibition or the latest show.

> *Here's an idea for you...*
>
> Don't be too picky. Okay, so you haven't fancied everyone who has been inviting you out. Well, get together with them anyway. Firstly, do you honestly prefer the excitement of being at home doing laundry? Secondly, you never know who they know. Thirdly, you might just find they're far more attractive than you originally realised once you've got to know them a little better.

- *Ditch the party expectations.* Parties may be a prime source of new dates, but don't go to them all pumped up in anticipation that you'll meet your dreamboat. Your hopes are sure to be dashed. Lower those expectations and recognise parties as an opportunity for good company, a dance or two and a chance to dress up in your finery.
- *Only fools play it cool.* If you look frosty and your body language says 'I am blowing this joint in five minutes if things don't liven up', people aren't exactly going to be enthusiastic about coming up to meet you, are they? Give them a little encouragement – smile, show interest. Catch their eye and hold their gaze. Signal loud and clear you'd welcome their approach.
- *Why 'Hi' is the best chat-up line ever.* It may be simple but it works brilliantly. According to statistics, a staggering 71% of men report they successfully meet women just by going up to them and saying 'Hi'. So, get back to basics and give it a try. Chances are you'll soon find yourself in conversation with someone who has attracted your notice.

I like her because she smiles at me and means it. **Anonymous**

How did it go?

Q. I've been waiting in a restaurant for half an hour and it's starting to look like my date has stood me up. How can I lessen the humiliation?

A. It's impossible not to take it personally when someone stands you up. Stay in control and give them a courteous call. You may feel they don't deserve the benefit of the doubt but err on the side of civility. If there is no reply, leave a polite note with the restaurant staff just in case something genuinely unforeseen has happened. You won't want to see your date again and it might feel like a hollow victory but you have done the right thing. A good chat with a supportive buddy will help lessen the sting.

Q. Friends say I sometimes come on too strong and scare off potential dates. Any suggestions?

A. The more outrageously you flirt, the more desperate you can look. Less is more when it comes to the fine art of seduction. Maintain intermittent eye contact; we're looking for glances that are warm and open – not prolonged and starry. Coy smiles and a raised eyebrow or two are so intriguing. Touch should be light and infrequent. Too much too soon is a real turn off. Flattery plays a key role in unlocking hearts but don't fawn. Ambiguous jokes are fine, but make sure humour isn't too raunchy or you'll sound sexually rapacious or even offensive. You know when you've got it right and you're on a fun journey together.

Networking

The end...

Or is it a new beginning?

We hope that these ideas will have helped you get all fired up and ready for business success. Whether you were looking for ideas on how to get over the shyness that's holding you back, needed to know where to find like-minded business people or wanted insider tips on climbing the ladder in your chosen career we hope this book has given you some useful pointers.

So why not let us know about it? Tell us how you got on. What did it for you – which ideas really made a difference to your business success or career prospects? Maybe you've got some tips of your own that you'd like to share. And if you liked this book you may find we have even more brilliant ideas that could help change other areas of your life for the better.

You'll find the Infinite Ideas crew waiting for you online at www.infideas.com.

Or if you prefer to write, then send your letters to:
Networking
Infinite Ideas Ltd
36 St Giles, Oxford, OX1 3LD, United Kingdom

We want to know what you think, because we're all working on making our lives better too. Give us your feedback and you could win a copy of another **52 Brilliant Ideas** book of your choice. Or maybe get a crack at writing your own.

Good luck. Be brilliant.

Offer one

Cash in your ideas
We hope you enjoy this book. We hope it inspires, amuses, educates and entertains you. But we don't assume that you're a novice, or that this is the first book that you've bought on the subject. You've got ideas of your own. Maybe our author has missed an idea that you use successfully. If so, why not send it to yourauthormissedatrick@infideas.com, and if we like it we'll post it on our bulletin board. Better still, if your idea makes it into print we'll send you four books of your choice or the cash equivalent. You'll be fully credited so that everyone knows you've had another Brilliant Idea.

Offer two

How could you refuse?
Amazing discounts on bulk quantities of Infinite Ideas books are available to corporations, professional associations and other organisations.

For details call us on:
+44 (0)1865 514888
Fax: +44 (0)1865 514777
or email: info@infideas.com

Where it's at...

Note: page references in **bold** type take you to Defining ideas and Here's an idea for you sections.

Academy for Chief Executives (ACE), 207
Ackerman, Jane, 119
agents, 53
aggressive behaviour, 86–7, 105, 162
alcohol consumption, 191, 192, 228–9
alumni networks, 178, 179
apologies, **225**
appearance, 50, 77–80, 88, 111, 189–90
  evening dress, 78–9
  over emphasis on, 229
Armstrong, Paul, 32–3
art appreciation, 138, 177
assertiveness, 31, 54, 124

B2B (business-to-business) and B2C (business-to-customer), 9
'beauty parades', 13
behaviour *see* manners
Bennett, Bo, 114
blankers, 42, 82
blogging, 73, 75, 208
body-language, 89–92, **199**

bosses, 38–9, 54
  insecure, 87, 124
  offended, 88, 220
  who take your credit, 87
brand building, **6**, 6–7, 9, 177
Brown, Rita Mae, 136
business cards, 65, 112
business coaches, 58
Butler, Jane, 144

Cabot, Stephanie, 126–7
Caine, Michael, 108
career service departments, 156
Carluccio, Priscilla and Antonio, 186
Carnegie, Dale, 69, 96
celebrations, 181–4
Chamber of Commerce, 121–4
charitable giving, 151–4
China, 1, 12
Christmas parties, 189–92
ClaimID, 73
Clinton, Bill, 94–5
clubs, 196, 207
cold calls, 66–70, 198–9
Comaford-Lynch, Christine, 19–20
communication
  'broken record technique', 31
  flattery, 85–8
  getting past the personal assistant, 22, 70

helping ditherers, 133
'hovering with intent', **21**, 92
listening, 48–9, 62, 91, **113**
methods and techniques, 17, 63–4, 113
telephoning, 17, 22, 68–70, 83, 198–9
town to country, **173**
using an interpreter, 173
with hard-of-hearing, 154
with overseas contacts, 173, 175
see also introductions; manners
Community Service Volunteers, 154
company returns, 26
competitors, 26, **118**, 119, 196
confidence *see* self-confidence
conflict, defusing, 86–7, 204, 227
Congdon, Amanda, 72
Conran, Terence, 186
contact management programs, 96
contacts
  brain picking, 126–7
  cold calls, 66–70, 198–9
  deleting information on, 97
  face-to-face, **28**, **139**, **199**
  following up new, 114

235

keeping in touch, 112–13, 171, 178, 209
pooling information on, 97
remembering personal details, 94–7, **95**, 99, 113
taking care of, **99**, 99–101
types, 42–6
unwelcome, 219
control, 143–4
corporate world, 13
business coaches, 58
dress codes, 77–80
embracing the culture, 142–5
events, 138–9, 141, 176–9
in-house networking, 29–30, 130–3
reorganisation, 120
researching, 23–4, 26, 200
see also work place
Coutts, 176–7
creative industries, 78
credit checks, 165
CVs, 166

D'Angelo, Anthony J., 200
Department of Trade and Industry, 26
difficult people, 43–6
discretion, 85–8, 202–5, 217
displacement activities, 92
drama classes, 4, 50, 91

Ecademy, 122
emails, 82, 113, 115, 203
entertaining, 147–50, 176–9

etiquette, international, 172–5
events
celebrations, 181–4
corporate world, 138–9, 141, 176–9
parties, 189–92, 230
preparing for, 34, 61–5, 139, 187
small business, 179
speakers, 209
teambuilding, 130–3, **131**
exit strategies, 220–3

Facebook, 167, 216
Family Business Network, **103**
family businesses, **103**, 103–5
sibling rivalry, 105
family chains, 14, 102–5
50 Cent, 6
financial services, 165
flat sharing, 227
Ford, Henry, 132
franchises, 13
Friedman, Vanessa, 79
friendships, 14–15, 107–8
funerals, 182, 184

Gates, Bill, 19–20
'Get Safe Online', 219
gifts, 98–101, 174
Gingrich, Newt, 208
gossiping, 202–5
beneficial, **203**, 205
government funded business networks, 33

greetings and goodbyes, 183
head-hunters, 78, 168–71
heroes *see* role models
high-rollers, 193–6
hobbies *see* sports and hobbies

Ibarra, Herminia, 30
identity theft, 215–9
image consultants, 79
inhibitions, 2, 10–11, 35, 182
getting-over them, 4, 61–5
initiative taking, **118**, **122**, **131**, 162
Institute for Family Business, **103**
intelligence gathering, 23–6, 199–200
international relations, 172–5
for women, 174
internet sites
blogging, 73, 75, 208
caution using, 164–7, 215–19
creating a presence, 71–5, **72**, **169**
e-mentoring, **58**, 145
emails, 82, 113, 115, 203
Google return results, 73
head-hunters, 169, **169**
online networking, 24, 122, 125, 145, 167, 215–19
websites, 23–6, **25**, **52**, 73–4, 209, 219
see also networking groups
internships, 159–62
introductions, **15**, 61–2, 83, 115, 123, 230

Index

new team members, 133
see also communication
investment clubs, 13

Jackson, Jesse, 53
Jacobs, Paul, 83
James, William, 226
Japan, 174
Jobling, Michele, 58
Joseph, Keith, 60

Kearney, AT, 177

language, 81–2
Lench, Sharon, 166, 218
Li, David, 12
liars, 205
life-coaches *see* mentoring
Lions, The, 121
lunches, 112, 147–50
    dining abroad, 173

Madonna, 6
Malloy, Edward A., 157
management consultancy, 78, 177–8
manipulators, 43–4, 184
manners, 81–4, 231
    accepting compliments, **182**
    avoiding offensive behaviour, 88, 225–6
    greetings and goodbyes, 183
    international etiquette, 172–5
    looking after guest speakers, 209
    remembering personal details, 94–7, **95**

thanking, 31, 98–101, **113**, 174, 192
treating others well, 106–7, 227
see also communication
marketing, 5–8
    brand building, **6**, 6–7, 177
    for students, 9
    public relations, 78, 171
    soft sell, 47–50
Mauss, Marcel, 100
McCartney, Stella, 103
McKay, Dawn Rosenberg, 191
meetings, 83–4, 91, **194**
    taking notes after, 95–6
mentoring, 56–60, 124, **126**, 145
Montoya, Peter, 8
MySpace, 167, 216

nepotism, 102–5
networking
    as natural habitat, 32–5
    as natural instinct, 1–4, 37–41
    high-octane, 193–6
    internet sites, 24, 122, 125, 145, 167, 215–19
    results, 17, **39**, 46, 101
    techniques, 111–15, 198–201
    the right mind-set, 10–13
    through sports and hobbies, 16, 139–41
    to suit women, 176
    where to start, 33–4, 128
    with your neighbours, 224–7
    with your spouse, 185–8, 190
    see also networking groups

networking groups
    alumni, 178, 179
    clubs and societies, 157, 196
    collaborations, 128
    contact programme, 207–8
    government funded, 33
    right model, 206–7
    starting your own, 125–8, 141
    trade associations, 121–4
    types, 14–16, **103**
    see also internet sites; networking
Norman, Barry, 104

online networking, 24, 122, 125, 145, 167, 215–19
'Get Safe Online,' 219

Parsloe, Eric, 59
parties, 189–92, 230
personal assistants, 22, 70, 108
Peters, Mark, 195
Peters, Tom, 7
Power, Penny, 64, 127
presentation *see* appearance; self-projection
presentations, 88, 134–7
    dos and don'ts, 136–7
    guest speakers, 209
    see also self-projection
presents, 98–101
press conferences, 200
prioritisation, 112
private banks, 176–7, 194–5
public relations, 78, 171
public speaking *see* presentations
publication, 137, 171

questioning, 201

recommendations, 51–4, 170
  testimonials, **107**, 109
recruitment, 21, 109, 155–8
  head-hunters, 78, 168–71
  web checks, 165
rejection, 210–13, 231
reliability, 27–8
reputation building, 106–9, 117–8
  recommendations, 51–4, **107**
  representing the company informally, **118**, **122**
  see also self-projection
research, 23–6, 199–200
Reynolds-Lacy, June, 21
Rockefeller, J.D., 161
Rodenberg, Patsy, 91
role models, 19–22
  parental, 102–4
Rolodex, 96
romance, 228–31
Rotary International, 122

Sandburg, Carl, 144
Saroyan, William, 212
Scoble, Robert, 73
secretaries see personal assistants
self-confidence, 3, 46
  asking questions, 201
  assertiveness, 31, 54, 124
  connecting with yourself, 91, **91**, **211**
  having your say, **135**
  inhibitions and, 2, 4, 10–11, 35, 61–5, 182
  insecure bosses and, 87
  marketing and, 47–50
  reliability and sincerity, 27–9, 41
  spouses and, 185–8, 190
  volunteering and, 151–4
  when you're over-dressed, 80
self-help books, 228
self-projection, 4
  corporate teambuilding and networking, 130–3
  web sites, 75
  see also presentations; reputation building
sexism, 84, 141, 192
small businesses, **103**, 103–5, 179,
socialising, 21
  building a reputation, 107–8
  Christmas parties, 189–92
  lunches, 112, 147–50
  mixing business with pleasure, 16, 41, 139–40
  preparing for, 34, 61–5, 115, 187
  romance and, 229–30
  with your spouse, 185–8, 190
Somerville, Stephen, 138, 177
sports and hobbies, 16, 139–41
spouses, 185–8, 190
stress, 143–4
students, 9, 15
  meeting role models, 20–1
  recruitment, 21, 155–8

university career services, 156
work experience, 156–8, **157**
work placements and internships, 159–62

tact, 85–8, 202–5, 217
teamwork, 118, 126, 128
  introducing new members, 133
  teambuilding events, 130–3, **131**
  with your spouse, 185–8, 190
telephoning, 17
  cold calling, 68–70, 198–9
  getting past the personal assistant, 22, 70
  mobile turn-offs, 83
testimonials, **107**, 109
thanking, 31, 98–101, **113**, 174, 192
Thompson, Dianne, 170
time management, 112, 142–5, **194**
trade associations, 121–4

universities, services and societies, 156, 157

voice training, 4
voluntary organisations, 4, **52**, 121, 151–4
  Community Service Volunteers, 154

238

Index

websites, **52**, 209
    researching through, 23–6, **25**
    services, 73–4, 219
work experience, 156–7, **157**
work placements, 159–60
work place
    building up skills, 151–4

colleagues, 15
CVs, 166
exit interviews, 223
exit strategies, 220–3
getting fired, 210–13
looking for a move, 52–4, 116–20, 126–7, 195

see also corporate world
work placements, 159–62
World Economic Forum, 193–4, 196
Wuillamie, Christiane, 107